THE LIFE STORY OF
C. I. SCOFIELD

by
CHARLES GALLAUDET TRUMBULL

DISPENSATIONAL
PUBLISHING HOUSE, INC.

Revived Classics
Series

ISBN: 978-1-945774-03-4

Dispensational Publishing House, Inc.
220 Paseo del Pueblo Norte
Taos, NM 87571

www.dispensationalpublishing.com

Ordering Information: Quantity sales. Special discounts are available on quantity purchases by churches, associations, and others. For details, contact the publisher at the address above or at our toll-free number: 1-844-321-4202

Orders by U.S. trade bookstores and wholesalers. Please contact the publisher: 1-844-321-4202

1 2 3 4 5 6 7 8 9 10

Dr. Scofield at work in the Library at Princeton

Table of Contents

REINTRODUCING SCOFIELD

D r. C.I. Scofield changed America. He, along with a faithful band of theological brothers, changed the way America (and much of the Western world) thinks. By taking a unique (and then popular) method of Biblical interpretation and integrating it into the printed Scriptures, he gave America its first "carry-everywhere" systematic theology.

That is, Dr. Scofield practically invented the ubiquitous *study Bible*.

While the Scofield Bible was not the first Bible with supplementary resources, it was the first modern study Bible and the first to be widely carried. The first Bible to contain cross references, maps and other aids was the Geneva Bible, first published in 1560. Scofield came along in 1909 and added extensive but not overwhelming explanatory notes on important passages, along with an extensive cross-reference system. I think that the cross-reference system alone is worth the purchase price of a *Scofield Reference Bible*. The reference system is a ready-made Bible study on so many of the important Bible topics. Just pick a topic, find where it begins in the chain-reference system, and follow it through the pages of the Bible. Soon you will have a systematic Biblical overview of that topic.

Not only Scofield's reference system, but the introductions to each book of the Bible and the notes on key passages, along with the in-text outline of dispensationalism, brought dispensational theology to the lower shelf, where it was within reach of the American church-going public. If your family has a heritage of church attendance, chances are that your parents or their parents had a well-worn *Scofield Bible*.

The pages which follow present Scofield in a positive light. They are, in a sense, an authorized biography. Undoubtedly, as in any such biography, if one wanted to know the full story he or she would have to dig further. This biography says very little about the difficult days of Scofield's early life, days in which he struggled with alcohol, had a marriage that ended in divorce and generally lived a wasted life. In this way, Scofield's life is a testimony to God's grace. And, in this way, Scofield's life is like so many of our own: There are parts of it we would not want to print. So, when you meet Scofield in these pages, you will know you are meeting the best parts of the man who made a very positive impact on our culture. Is there more to the story? Certainly so. Scofield requested and received discharge from the Confederate Army (he was living in Texas and was considered an *alien friend*). He also served in the Kansas legislature and the United States District Attorney's office, but left in scandal. He later divorced and left two daughters, and possibly even spent some time in jail, and in 1879 was converted under the ministry of D.L. Moody (whose church he would later pastor). Yes, there is so much more to the story than what you read in these pages.

The author of this book, Charles G. Trumbull, may also be an odd choice for the biography of one like Scofield. Trumbull was the influential editor of *The Sunday School Times*, a publication which originally ran from 1859 to 1966, and an influence in the once-powerful American Sunday School Union. (Trumbull's father, Henry Clay Trumbull, was one of the pioneers of the Sunday School movement in America.) Charles Trumbull wrote many books and was influential in bringing the Keswick movement to the United States. Keswick is the Higher Life movement, which would be rejected by many dispensationalists today.

But the fact remains that C.I. Scofield took a then-popular theological system and made it part of the fabric of American life. At Dispensational Publishing House, our desire is to take the theological system he taught and re-teach it to a society that has forgotten its truths. Dispensationalism has a bad reputation today in the eyes of many. Few seminaries give it any respect—let alone teach it with academic integrity. But dispensationalism is a method of Biblical interpretation that is worthy of consideration, and those who toss it out based on its caricature rather than its character are missing a great deal of spiritual blessing and Biblical understanding.

When I stand in the pulpit, I use a *Scofield Reference Bible* (the 1917 edition). I do not agree with all of Scofield's notes, but I do think all of his notes are worthy of digging into. When we read his notes, we should *question the assumptions* against the text of the only infallible source, the Word of God. But when I stand with my *Scofield Bible*, I know that I am standing with a piece of American Christian history. It popularized a system of theology that I hold, and it shaped "The Greatest Generation" in its theological mindset. It brought systematized theological thought to the masses.

And for that, I remain grateful.

Randy White, D.Min.
Founder and CEO
Dispensational Publishing House, Inc.

THE
LIFE STORY
OF
C. I. SCOFIELD

By
CHARLES GALLAUDET TRUMBULL

Editor of "The Sunday School Times,"
Author of "Taking Men Alive," "Messages for the Morning Watch,"
"What Is the Gospel?" etc.

NEW YORK
OXFORD UNIVERSITY PRESS
AMERICAN BRANCH: 35 WEST 32ND STREET
LONDON, TORONTO, MELBOURNE AND BOMBAY

Copyright 1920

by

Oxford University Press American Branch

Trumbull, Charles Gallaudet. The Life Story of C. I. Scofield. New York;

London; Toronto; Melbourne; Bombay: Oxford University Press, 1920. Print.

1

HOW THE TRAINING BEGAN

A SMALL BOY lay flat on his stomach before an open fireplace. He was not watching the fire; he was poring over a book. It was not a boys' book, either; there were few such then, and they were not in the small library of a frontier home. He was reading Shakespeare. If you had come upon him at another time, in the same position and place, you would have found it was history. The home library held nothing frivolous, and he devoured all he found.

The youngster had a genuine passion for knowledge. When he reached the age of twelve he began to make a chart of universal history! His sisters laughed at him for it; but he kept right on. It was not finished in a day or a week, that chart; he had to remake it every now and then, as he discovered that he had left out a whole country or an entire historical epoch! But he kept at it until it was finished, down to the American Revolution, which was his terminus.

This boy was a great hunter—a hunter through the pages of books. When he found mention of a certain person in his reading, he would hunt through all other volumes that he could lay hold of until he had found out more about that person. For example, he would come across a reference to one Alexander, son of Philip of Macedon. Philip—who was he? And where was Macedonia? There were two things he must run down. He kept after Philip and Macedonia until he knew something about both.

The reading of Greek history led to the reading of Greek litera-ture,—in translation, of course. Neighbors of his family learned of his interest and desire, and loaned him anything from their libraries that was grist to his mill.

The family were Episcopalians; rectors were pretty well-educated men, even in those days. The rector of the family of this boy was a cultured Englishman, a graduate of Rugby and Oxford; and he gladly helped the boy to all the good reading that he had. And so, with eager mind, the boy kept on digging in books to get learning. His unusual habit of hunting out and running down information concerning whatever he came across trained him in thoroughness. He felt that he must get things at first hand.

The boy's father and mother were true Christians, old-fash-ioned believers. His father read the Bible to him and encouraged him to read it for himself. The father was not "instructed" in the full range of Biblical truth, but he lived very much in the Book of Psalms, and loved David greatly. And the boy read his Bible lessons, like any other boy in a respectable Christian family; but he did not dream that the Bible was a book to be studied like other books, and he gave it little attention. Yet what a preparation he was getting, all unconsciously, in mental habits of thoroughness and of verification and of first-hand study, all of which make for scholarship, for the producing, years later, of the Reference Bible for which hundreds of thousands now love and honor his name!

Was the mother an influence in the life of this boy and man? She died soon after his birth: died as a result of bringing him into the world. Perhaps some might think that that answers the question in the negative. But as the mother lay dying, the new-born baby boy by her side, she prayed for him, and asked God that he might be a minister of the Gospel of Jesus Christ. When the boy grew up he was not told this; the father, with a strict sense of honor, told the sisters that young Cyrus must not be told of his mother's prayer lest he be unduly influenced by it, and enter upon a life-calling simply because of sentiment and from a sense of obligation to a dying mother's wish. Only after that boy had accepted the call to the ministry and had become, indeed, an ambassador of Christ was he told of his mother's prayer. Yes, God hears and answers prayer.

It was amid the chivalry, the bravery, the honor, the old-school standards of gentleman and gentlewoman of the South before the Civil War that the boy was doing his omnivorous reading and forming his study habits. His family then were living in Tennessee. He had been born in the woods of Michigan, in Lenawee County. Pure American Colonial ancestry was his. One of the earliest sounds he can remember is that of the crash of falling trees in the forest. There in that open-air, pioneer life he came to love the woods, and the birds, and animal life of every sort. He has never lost that love. He has it to-day with an intensity that might surprise some.

In spite of his prodigious love for study, the youngster was a real boy, doing the things other real boys do. He had four sisters, but was the only surviving son in the family, two others having died before his birth. One day, when a little chap six or eight years old, he felt that his many sisters were shamefully neglecting him; so "Bub"—as his sisters called him—and a little friend decided to run away from home.

They traveled all day, and at nightfall they encountered some wood-choppers who hospitably asked them to spend the night before their great log fire. The following morning, somehow, the youngsters did not go farther, but retraced their steps, dirty-faced and homesick. Their stomachs had a sense of need, too; so they decided to stop at a farm-house and ask for something to eat. This they did at several farm-houses, but could not get up courage to ask for more than a drink of water, hoping each time that there might be an accompanying cookie. Nothing but water came their way.

Finally the two little runaways reached home. No special welcome awaited them, for the sisters had decided that they would act as though nothing unusual had happened. The son of the family was quite nonplussed, having expected an enthusiastic welcome.

The biographer is glad to record, however, that the boy's father took him on his lap and gave him an extra tight hug, much to the boy's delight. And years afterward the father told him that he had not slept a wink that night when his "wandering boy" was not under the home roof with him.

It was August 19, 1843, that Cyrus Ingerson Scofield was born. Part of the family moved to Tennessee while he was a young boy, and that Southern State was his home until he was seventeen. The slavery of that region was of a mild, kindly, patriarchal form. Like so many others in the South, masters and mistresses and slaves loved one another. When, after the war, some of these Southern families returned to their homes, and found not only no homes, but the farms and the very fences burned down by the armies, with nothing left but the land itself, the old slaves were sometimes found still living there, free, but desperately poor. And more than one Southern family mortgaged its land in order to continue to take care of its free but needy slaves.

The men of the Southland with whom young Scofield was brought up, while not religious as a rule, had a profound respect for anything called religion; they cherished a very high sense of honor; they were truthful, and they were brave. This led sometimes to the foolish practice of dueling; but the standards back of it all made a deep impression on the boy.

Going on with his studies at the family home near Lebanon, Wilson County, Tennessee, he was making his plans to pass the examinations for entrance to the university. But just at this time the Civil War came on and all Southern schools were closed. Enlisting at once, though only seventeen, he had a four years' course in another kind of college than that which he had anticipated. He set to work as soon as the war was over; and thus it was that he never had a formal collegiate or academic education. But how much greater an education had he acquired, both before and after those years when he had expected to be within college walls, than many a college graduate! And from that day to this he has never lost his love for study and his desire for knowledge.

Young Scofield had gone into the Confederate Army, as a matter of course, with his boyhood friends and associates. Though not seventeen, he was a big fellow, tall, strong, though slender, and practically never sick in his life. "Raised on a horse," he was a perfect horseman, and naturally enough he was often called upon for orderly work. Learning how to carry vital messages, scrawled on a scrap of paper with the pommel of a saddle as a writing-desk, while shells and bullets were falling, gave him a disciplinary training in carrying through difficult commissions. His position as orderly, while he continued as only an enlisted man throughout the war, threw him constantly with the officers and others constituting the staff, with all the influences and associations that this would mean to an impressionable boy.

Before he was nineteen young Scofield had been under fire in eighteen battles and minor engagements. The Cross of Honor was awarded to him for bravery at Antietam. He was twelve miles from Appomattox when Lee surrendered to Grant. Dr. Scofield to-day enjoys telling the incident of Lee's having said to Grant, after the surrender, that inasmuch as Grant's armies had cut the

Confederates off from their supplies, their men were in need of food; and he asked if the Northern commander would be so kind as to issue an order permitting the bringing of food from the Southern supply trains to the men. Grant replied that he did not know where Lee's supplies were, but he did know where the Union supplies were, and he would at once issue an order that the Confederate soldiers be cared for from the Union supplies—as he promptly did. And young Private Scofield was careful to get his share of those Union "eats," as he says with emphasis.

His life was not destined to be ended in that conflict. He was not twenty-two when the war was over; and he went to live in St. Louis, the home of his eldest sister. She had married into one of the best Creole or French families of the South; and there the young fellow was plunged into the French society of that great city.

St. Louis was then the great fur market of the world for original, uncured fur. And the rapid growth of the city was making million-aires of some of the French people there. Scofield read and studied French, which was freely used as the language of Creole society in St. Louis in those days; he still uses the language in his reading. The influences of the European, extremely formal social life of that day were entering into his impressionable years also.

His sister's husband, a man of wealth and high social standing and leadership, told young Scofield that he would back him in any line of profession or life-work he might choose to take up. They talked over different professions together, and it came out that the practice of law seemed the most attractive. Having settled this, the question arose as to how the young man would prepare for his coveted life-work. The brother-in-law had told him to call upon him for whatever assistance he needed. It was a time of test and of real struggle. But the younger man met it by telling his brother that, while he thanked him ten thousand times for his generous offer to help, he believed it was best for him to work things out for himself and provide for his own education and support. He wanted to fight his own way; and he did so.

In order to get together money for his legal education, he started in at once as a clerk in an office for the examination of land titles—a line closely related to the law. This was a still further training of his mind for searching out things, and had its place in God's later plans for his life. After less than two years' work in this office, his devotion to this technical branch resulted in his appointment as chief clerk, being chosen from among the considerable number of young men in the office. This gave him a good salary. Now he made his plans to enter upon the actual study of law in one of the best law offices in St. Louis. That city had then, as for many years, a remarkably strong bar. It was a treat for the young law student to go into court and hear the able, brainy men of that day.

While still pursuing his law studies, and before being admitted to the bar, a very extensive and involved lawsuit in connection with the landholdings in Kansas of his brother-in-law's family was begun; and the family asked young Scofield to let them put the matter into his hands for his personal charge and direction. He protested, saying that he had not the experience or ability to undertake this. They would not accept his declination, but insisted upon his assuming the responsibility in their behalf, telling him to retain the best lawyers he pleased to insure the necessary legal skill. Yielding to their urgent request, he went at the task in his old way of studying things out and making sure of bringing all the facts together. Then he put this material into the hands of his lawyers,—and among the brilliant lawyers retained by him for this great case was John J. Ingalls. Scofield's lawyers won the case.

II

NAMING INGALLS FOR THE SENATE

THE life of C. I. Scofield up to the time of his conversion is chiefly of interest as having fallen within times of permanent historic import in which he bore a characteristically American part.

The Scofield family is well-born and is traced back for centuries to its English forebears. Indeed, one of the Scofield ancestors fought a duel with that ancestor of the poet Byron who was called "the wicked" Lord Byron. And in a volume noted as Oxford Grants I, now in the Herald's College, London, is found the following:

"To All and Singuler etc.: Forasmuch as Cuthbert Scofeld of Scofeld in Countie of Lancaster, Esquire, sonne and heire of James Scofeld, well borne and descended of worthy progenitors such as have of longe tyme used and boren armes as apt and significant tokens of their race and gentry, ...

"In witnesse whereof, I the said Norroy Kinge of Armes have heereunto subscribed my name this sixt day of March, in the yere of our Lord God 1582 and in the 25 yere of the reigne of our most gracious souveigne Lady Queen Elizabeth."

As you enter the doorway of "Greyshingles," the Scofield home at Douglaston, Long Island, you see on the wall at the right a quaint pen-and-ink sketch of an old English building, showing moat, and bridge, and heavy oaken door. The Scofield coat of arms is there, and the sketch bears the inscription:

"Scofield Hall, erected 1550, Rochdale, Lancashire, England, from a sketch in Raines MSS., British Museum."

Thus of Colonial and Revolutionary ancestry, so strongly Puritan that, from Daniel Scofield the immigrant (1639) to and including himself, every man and woman in the chain of descent bore a Bible name—usually chosen from the Old Testament—he was born, very properly for an American boy, in the depths of a Western forest. For the West was in its winning, and the grandfather and father of that woodland baby owned large acres of primeval trees in Lenawee County, Michigan. They had built a dam across the Raisin River and erected a sawmill; but so much was it still a wilderness that little Scofield's grandmother had to defend her very life against a drunken Indian, and his father's unerring rifle slew a wild-cat that was bearing to her hungry brood a baby stolen from a frontier crib. Into such a life little Scofield was born.

And then came the first of the dramatic changes of which young Scofield's life was so full. A removal took the boy of the Michigan settlement to pass, as it turned out, the formative years of his early life in the absolutely contrasted life of middle Tennessee during the last years of the slavery régime—absolutely contrasted, and yet no less intensely and characteristically American. It was among a Whig aristocracy, educated, wealthy (for that time and region), of easy, hospitable life, and of a plain democratic commonalty, honest, truthful, brave; who owned few slaves but tilled the soil in manly independence, keeping in their fat pastures blooded horses and herds of high-bred cattle. It is safe to say that no people ever surpassed these in the great primitive virtues of courage, integrity, and kindliness. Their accomplishments were to ride and shoot, and their intellectual interests were politics and sectarian religion.

The Civil War was the next dramatic chapter in his life. Those years in an atmosphere created by the great personalities of Lee and Jackson furnished an indelible lesson in his training. And then came his removal to St. Louis and his preparation for the profession of law, begun by disciplinary training in a land office, as has been narrated, and hastened by the great lawsuit of his brother-in-law's family, of which he was asked to take charge.

It became necessary for young Scofield to remove to Kansas, where the land interests involved in the Loisel family lawsuit were situated. Here he was urged to let his name be offered for admission to the bar; he underwent the severe ordeal of those days, being examined by the three lawyers in open court to whom his examination was formally assigned, and also being asked questions, as was the custom, by any judges and members of the bar present. Having passed this stiff examination, he was, when about twenty-six years of age, admitted to the bar.

Then the people of Atchison, Kansas, elected him to the State legislature. After two years of experience as a young legislator, serving as chairman of its Judiciary Committee, he removed to Nemaha County, where the Loisel lawsuits were pending, and here he was again and at once elected to the legislature.

It will be remembered that the long and acrimonious discussion of the attempt to include the Territory of Kansas within the number of States in which slaves might be held had brought into that Territory an unusual number of the ablest young men from both the North and the South—a fact which invested life in the young State with peculiar interest. Every possible issue was discussed down to the final word, though the heat engendered by the slavery discussion had ceased with the ending of the Civil War.

Among the ablest and best-trained of the young men who had been drawn to Kansas by the slavery agitation was John James

Ingalls, of Atchison, graduate of Williams College, a natural wit and orator, and with whom young Scofield was associated in the Loisel land case.

Then occurred an event that arrested in a singular degree the attention of the nation.

The senior United States Senator from Kansas, Samuel C. Pomeroy, had become notorious through land-corruption deals. His term in the Senate was expiring, and he was a candidate for re-election. Young Scofield, like some others, was satisfied that Pomeroy was buying votes. A small but earnest anti-Pomeroy element of State legislature men were holding a series of meetings in a hall in the State capital, Topeka. Their leader came to Scofield one afternoon and asked him bluntly where he stood on Pomeroy's re-election.

"Against Pomeroy," was the prompt reply.

The anti-Pomeroy man was interested, and said he wanted to talk freely with Scofield. Then he asked the question, "Have you a man to nominate in his place?"

"Yes," came the reply again: "John J. Ingalls. But," added Scofield, "I don't want to see Ingalls nominated, just to have him defeated."

At this the anti-Pomeroy man answered earnestly, "I *know* that *Pomeroy* will be defeated. Will you, without asking any questions, take my word for this?"

Scofield thought it over for a moment, and said he would. He wired to Ingalls to come over to the capital, which was done by engaging a special train to bring him. Immediately upon his arrival he and Scofield conferred together. Scofield laid the facts as fully before his older friend as he could. Ingalls was impressed, and after earnest conference he asked the younger man, "What do you advise?"

"You ought to do it," came the reply.

Ingalls said frankly that he did not believe his election was possible under the circumstances; but he was ready to follow the counsel of his friends; and he authorized him to say that he, Ingalls, would accept the anti-Pomeroy nomination.

The anti-Pomeroy leader had told Scofield that their group were going to remain in session through the night preceding the election, not leaving the hall, and even having their breakfasts brought in, in order to see the matter through. At one o'clock in the morning Scofield entered the hall where they were meeting, with Mr. Ingalls on his arm. Ingalls, a fine-looking, tall, slender man, then made a powerful address for clean politics in Kansas. The entire group had their breakfast together, and went over in a body to the House of Representatives.

The Pomeroy cohort had already assembled. A little later the senators marched in. The Lieutenant-Governor, as was the custom, presided.

Mr. Pomeroy was nominated to succeed himself as Senator of the United States, in a speech in which his "great services" to the State of Kansas were fully rehearsed.

Then Senator York, the leader of the anti-Pomeroy forces, rose to his feet, deathly white. Scofield looked at him, and was afraid he would not be able even to use his voice, so overcome by emotion did he seem. But in a moment, to the utter amazement of all who heard him, he said: "Mr. President, I rise to second the nomination of S. C. Pomeroy." [Representative Scofield was not then a converted man, and he decided then and there that after the meeting he would take the senator outside and thrash him.] "But," went on Senator York, reaching to his hip pocket, and drawing out a large bundle of something, "not to a seat in the United States Senate, but to a cell in the Kansas State Penitentiary at Leavenworth." He then called to his side one of the boy pages of the legislature, and continued: "Mr. President, I am sending you by the innocent hand of this boy seven thousand dollars in greenbacks that were handed me last night by S. C. Pomeroy for my vote."

The bundle of money was carried up to the desk of the Lieutenant-Governor, and there, in the presence of all, it was laid in plain sight upon a book. There was a silence like death over the entire hall of representatives.

In that strange silence Scofield rose and nominated John J. Ingalls to the United States Senate. Member after member rose to second the nomination.

The Lieutenant-Governor, his face tense with excitement, asked if there were any other nominations. None was offered. And then an amazing thing happened. The vote was taken; and *every vote cast was for John J. Ingalls.* Even the man who had nominated Pomeroy voted for Ingalls! And many another legislator there, with Pomeroy's money in his pocket, dared not do otherwise than repudiate his man and come out in the solid vote for decency and honesty.

There was another dead silence, as the presiding officer rose and, in a shaking voice, said: "Every ballot has been cast for John J. Ingalls. I hereby declare him duly elected Senator from Kansas for the United States."

There were shouts of "Ingalls! Ingalls!"

"Mr. Scofield, do you know where Mr. Ingalls is?" asked the Lieutenant-Governor. "Can you produce him?"

"I think I can, sir," answered young Scofield, "if the house will continue in session for twenty minutes."

He disappeared, and in five minutes he was back with Mr. Ingalls. Dazed by the suddenness and utter unexpectedness of the event, Mr. Ingalls made a brief address of acceptance of the nomination, amid the cheers of senators and legislators. And for eighteen years from that time Ingalls served in the United States Senate, through successive re-elections.

It is not surprising that General Grant, then President of the United States for his second term, appointed C. I. Scofield United States Attorney for the District of Kansas. That included not only the entire State of Kansas, but also what is now much of Oklahoma—then Indian Territory. The young legislator was the youngest United States attorney at that time in the United States— scarcely thirty years old. And the office that he held was particularly important, because the United States was then removing the roving Indians of the plains to fixed reservations, which meant unusual work for the District Attorney's office.

Among other things that the Government instructed United States District Attorney Scofield to do was to stop certain men who were taking whisky into Indian Territory and selling it to the Indians. Scofield secured an escort of cavalry and went after these men. He would have been shot down instantly by them if they could have done this. But he rounded up some of the worst men in this law-breaking liquor business, and brought them back to Leavenworth.

At the trial, necessarily most of the District Attorney's witnesses were Indians—and Indians who could not speak a word of English. It was a strange scene that went on in the court-room, as an uncouth-looking half-breed interpreted for the Indians. But the case proceeded, the defence for the liquor men trying in vain to break down the testimony of the Indians, and the Indians themselves made a favorable impression by their evident honesty, and respect, and reverence for the Great Spirit when the question of the nature of an oath came up, and it ended by the conviction of the liquor men.

When, later in the day, Scofield went to the lodgings where he had had his Indian witnesses entertained, he found the leading one, a stately chief named "Powder Face," squatting on a bed. As the District Attorney entered the room, the Indian quickly raised his left hand high over his head, with his right hand patted his heart, and smiled—and a smile is a very rare thing to see on the face of an Indian. What it meant was, "I love you." And the interpreter explained to Scofield, "Powder Face would die for you now, after making that sign. It is a pledge of eternal friendship."

III

WON TO CHRIST

THE political life into which young District Attorney Scofield now found himself plunged, by virtue of his Federal office and work, involved frequent trips from Kansas to Washington, and associations and activities that were not entirely to his liking. The profession of law was his life choice; his political work was interfering with that. He had, indeed, become very much dissatisfied with his own life; he was not living up even to his own ideals, unconverted man though he was. So after two years' service as United States District Attorney he resigned the office and returned to St. Louis to practise law.

The drinking, loose ways of the political crowd upon whom Scofield had now turned his back had not been to his liking, nevertheless he himself had been living not at all as a Puritan. The moderate use of liquor was a commonplace in the life in which he moved and had been reared. He drank as he pleased, and, like most men who drink "in moderation," he soon drank too much.

From 1865 until 1879 his life was intense, largely a life of combat in courts and politics which not seldom became extremely embittered. He says himself of that period: "It must not be forgotten or suppressed that the habit of drink during this period became fastened upon me, for it is due to my adorable Lord that His perfect and instantaneous deliverance of me should be made known, as I have testified again and again in meetings."

After taking up again in St. Louis the practice of law, a young man of about his own age, Thomas S. McPheeters, became one of his intimate friends. McPheeters was the son of a well-known minister and godly man of great influence, who was pastor of the First (Southern) Presbyterian Church of that city. Another son of that father is Prof. William M. McPheeters, of the Southern Presbyterian Theological Seminary at Columbia, S. C.

Scofield's father and mother had been true, old-fashioned believers. He was not. He had gone to Sunday-school as a boy because he was made to go. He hated to go; it made little impression upon him; and he learned little there. He heard many a sermon, but none that affected him in any way until after his conversion.

In his St. Louis law office, one day, McPheeters came to see him. After talking a while, McPheeters got up to go. With his hand upon the door-knob, he turned and faced Scofield, saying: "For a long time I have been wanting to ask you a question that I have been afraid to ask, but that I am going to ask now."

"I never thought of you as 'afraid,' " said Scofield in hearty friendship. "What is your question?"

"I want to ask you why you are not a Christian?" came the unexpected reply.

Now Thomas McPheeters was an outspoken Christian himself, utterly devoted to his Lord, and a real soul-winner, at the same time a society man in the best sense of that word, mingling with the best social life of his day. He and Scofield had much in common—except Christ.

The lawyer replied thoughtfully: "Does not the Bible say something about drunkards having no place in heaven? I am a hard drinker, McPheeters."

"You haven't answered my question, Scofield," the other man came back. "Why are you not a Christian?"

"I have always been a nominal Episcopalian, you know," said Scofield, "but I do not recall ever having been shown just how to be a Christian. I do not know how."

Now McPheeters had his answer. He drew up a chair, took a Testament out of his pocket, and read passage after passage from the precious Good News, plainly telling his friend how to be saved. "Will you accept the Lord Jesus Christ as your Saviour?" he asked.

"I'm going to think about it," said Scofield.

"No, you're not," answered McPheeters. "You've been thinking about it all your life. Will you settle it now? Will you believe on Christ now, and be saved?"

The logical-minded, clear-thinking lawyer liked clean-cut statements and unequivocal questions and answers. After a moment's thought he looked his friend full in the face, and said quietly, "I will." The two men dropped down on their knees together. Scofield told the Lord Jesus Christ that he believed on Him as his personal Saviour, and before he arose from his knees he had been born again: there was a new creation, old things had passed away, behold, all things had become new. Thomas S. McPheeters had been used of God to lead C. I. Scofield to Christ.

An old friend of McPheeters, Mr. J. L. Woodbridge, of Pueblo, Colorado, upon reading this incident, has written to the biographer:

"It was a privilege to know Mr. McPheeters, or Tom, as his friends knew him. Big in body and soul, he carried the Saviour about with him all the time; or, rather, the Saviour carried him. I know the account you give is accurate because it is just the way he would go about it. It seemed as if he could approach any man on earth on the subject with perfect confidence. His life was *all* the Christian life, in business as elsewhere. Welcome everywhere, to all classes, his genial frankness and *bonhomie* swept everything before it. We were fellow commissioners to the General Assembly of the Southern Presbyterian Church at Nashville in 1904, and in his speeches there his great magnetism affected the large audiences just as it did individuals. His influence, perpetuated through Dr. Scofield and thousands of others, will never die."

There have been all sorts of inaccurate and misleading stories of the conversion of Dr. Scofield. Passing from mouth to mouth, some of these have gained currency, and, as he says himself, he long ago gave up hope of denying or correcting them. But these facts have been given here as they actually occurred, and as Dr. Scofield wishes them to be known. Shortly before this chapter of the Life Story went to press in its serial publication, the writer received a letter from Dr. Scofield that he gladly incorporates here, so that many may rejoice in the marvel of its testimony:

"Such successes as I achieved in my life in the world of selfish aspiration might easily be made so prominent in my life story as to leave my conversion an event like the others. I owe it to the Lord and to my boundless indebtedness to His grace to do what I may to correct the notion that it was a brilliantly successful man who, in my person, came to Christ.

"Great opportunities had indeed been given me, and for years I made them my own. But slowly, insidiously, the all but universal habit of drink in the society and among the men of my time overmastered me. It was not a victor in the battle of life—though victories had come to him—but a ruined and hopeless man who, despite all his struggles, was fast bound in chains of his own forging. He had no thought of Christ other than a vague respect, the survival of a family influence. There was no hope that in a church some time he might hear and believe the Gospel, for he never went to church.

"And then Jesus Christ took up the case. Men were beginning

to turn away from him, but the Lord of glory sought him. Through Thomas McPheeters, a joyous, hopeful soul, Jesus Christ offered Himself to that wreck.

"It was a Bible conversion. From a worn pocket Testament McPheeters read to me the great Gospel passages, the great deliverance passages, John 3:16; 6:47; 10:28; Acts 13:38, 39, and the like. And when I asked, like the Philippian jailer of old, 'What must I do to be saved?' he just read them again, and we knelt, and I received Jesus Christ as my Saviour. And—oh! Trumbull, put it into the story, put it big and plain: instantly the chains were broken never to be forged again—the passion for drink was taken away. Put it 'Instantly,' dear Trumbull. Make it plain. Don't say: 'He strove with his drink-sin and came off victor.' He did nothing of the kind. Divine power did it, wholly of grace. To Christ be all the glory.

> "Yours in His love,
> "C. I. SCOFIELD."

The writer of this life story knows too well that no Christian ever, under any circumstances, "strove with his sin and came off victor," to suggest any such false interpretation as that for the victory of the Lord Jesus Christ in the life of this now veteran saint. The secret of Dr. Scofield's "Victorious Life" is the same and only secret of the Victorious Life of every believer, wherever such victory is experienced: he "let go, and let God'; he did not try to add his efforts to God's finished and perfect work. He yielded and believed: and the Captain of his Salvation, instantly making him more than conqueror, led him in triumph.

Lawyer Scofield was saved, and he knew it. For Thomas McPheeters knew the Gospel, and he had made it perfectly plain to his friend. There was no vagueness or uncertainty in McPheeters' appeal, nor in Scofield's acceptance. From that day to this he has never had any doubt that he was at that time, in the city of St. Louis, at thirty-six years of age, in the year 1879, born again through faith in the Son of God.

Christ came in, and drink went out. The miracle of the Victorious Life was instantly wrought for him and in him: he lost all desire for drink then and there. God took it. It was *gone*.

The man who has passed from death into life, from bondage into freedom, from defeat into victory, cannot help telling about it. More than once Dr. Scofield, after he had entered the ministry and was giving his whole life to Christian service, testified to his deliverance from the drink habit. And years later, when he was D. L. Moody's home pastor at Northfield, Mr. Moody, then his devoted friend, was led to speak to him about this, and advised against it. Mr. Moody said he had noticed that Dr. Scofield would from time to time, in his public messages, tell of his former bondage to drink and of his deliverance, and he said he believed he ought not to do this except in revival meetings where drinking men might be present: that any sin of that sort was in the past, under the blood of the Lord Jesus, and now solely a matter between God and Scofield, and not for the general public.

Dr. Scofield appreciated Mr. Moody's feeling, and, in giving full recognition to the suggestion, replied that of course Mr. Moody would recognize that he must leave himself in the hands of the Holy Spirit as to this, for whatever guidance He might indicate.

A short time after the conversation Dr. Scofield was speaking at Northfield, addressing an audience of about eight hundred Northfield students. And during the course of his address he was strongly led to give the testimony of his own deliverance, years before, from the power of drink, through the sufficiency of the

Lord Jesus Christ. God used his testimony that day mightily and blessedly in the lives of the students.

After the service was over, Mr. Moody went to Dr. Scofield and said, with characteristic impulsiveness and intensity: "Scofield, you take the advice of the Holy Spirit hereafter, and not of D. L. Moody."

After the young lawyer's conversion, McPheeters, now infinitely more his friend in Christ, brought him at once into association with strong Christian men. The St. Louis Young Men's Christian Association secretary at that time was Walter C. Douglas, the well-known Y. M. C. A. worker who was later the general secretary at Philadelphia, and who has had a long career of useful Christian service in this field. Douglas himself had been a lawyer, and after conversion had gone into Y. M. C. A. work; and he had come under the influence of Dr. James H. Brookes, the remarkable preacher, pastor, and Bible teacher of St. Louis. Scofield quickly got into Christian work and Y. M. C. A. service, and he was fortunate in securing the personal friendship of Dr. Brookes early in his Christian life. He got into the habit of going to the home of that Spirit-guided and illumined Bible teacher, and there studying the Bible under his direction.

There were probably few if any men of the last fifty years in North America who did as much to influence and guide the Bible study and Christian life of the sound Christian leaders of our generation as James H. Brookes. He was peculiarly blessed of God in making plain dispensational truth and the great fundamentals of the prophetic study of God's Word. To-day, more than forty years after Dr. Scofield first came under that remarkable man's influence, he says of him:

"James H. Brookes was the greatest Bible student I have ever known. His great strength lay in the fact that he held truth in balance—he always balanced whatever truth he was giving by some other truth; that is, whether he mentioned the other truth or not, he held it at least in his mind over against the truth that he was giving, and thus was kept from unbalanced or false emphasis.

"Dr. Brookes was an amazing blessing to me, but never more than in telling me this: 'There is no such thing in the Bible as an *abstract* proposition. Everything in the Bible is meant to be turned into life. It must first of all be grounded in doctrine. There is such a thing as experience which is real but which is not founded on Scripture; then it becomes either fanatical or a discouragement. Therefore, we are always to interpret experience by Scripture—never Scripture by experience. There is always in Scripture a doctrinal *basis*, and there is always in Scripture an account of an experience based on that doctrine; and this account is perfectly accurate because it is inspired.' "

A St. Louis man, C. E. Paxson, who made young Scofield's acquaintance at the Y. M. C. A. soon after his conversion, was seated in his own office one day with a brand-new Bible before him, which he was marking. Scofield came in, and seeing what he was doing, exclaimed, with consternation: "Why, man, you are spoiling that fine new Bible!"

For answer Mr. Paxson pointed him to the place in the eighth chapter of Acts where he had underscored the fifth verse, reading: "Then Philip went down to the city of Samaria, and preached Christ unto them." This he had connected by a light line with the eighth verse, which he had also underscored, reading, "And there was great joy in that city." Scofield saw the point at once, and became an advocate of Bible-marking. Many years after he was accustomed to greeting his friend Paxson with the words: "Here is the man who first taught me to mark my Bible."

When the young convert and Christian worker looked around

DR. JAMES H. BROOKES
Dr. Brookes was Dr. Scofeild's first Bible teacher. Of him to-day he says,
"He was the greatest Bible student I have ever known."

for a church home, he was led to join the Pilgrim Congregational Church, of which Dr. C. L. Goodell was pastor, making this choice because of the warmth of personal friendship that he had found in Dr. Goodell. Goodell and Brookes were great friends, and Dr. Brookes told Scofield that he believed he had done well in connecting himself with Dr. Goodell's church, "For," he said, "he is the greatest pastor I ever saw; and I'll see that you get the Bible teaching you need."

A man of Scofield's intensity, and natural leadership, and love of activity and expression could not keep still in his Christian life. He soon got to leading meetings, and even to preaching a little. He felt that the hand of the Lord was upon him.

His Y. M. C. A. friend, Walter Douglas, introduced the young converted lawyer to the president of one of the railroads that came into St. Louis, and asked the railroad man if Scofield might hold religious meetings for railroad men at East St. Louis, at the "bridge-head." This was where many trains and different roads came in before crossing the bridge to St. Louis proper; it was a locality infested with saloons, and with numbers of railroad men loafing around waiting the opportunity to take their own trains across.

The railroad president gave his cordial permission for the holding of such meetings; but those who knew of it were skeptical—the men wouldn't come, they said.

Scofield tried his hand at it, however, and he soon found that he could not make much headway in getting a hearing among the roistering, indifferent railroad men of that day. About that time he was led to befriend a railroad man who was sick. He saw to it that the sick man had a good doctor, and whatever else was needed. This Jim Turner, a freight conductor, not only found his health under Scofield's loving ministry, but he found his Saviour also. Then he went back to the tracks with his new friend Scofield; he would stand alongside and shout out a testimony for Christ, telling his railroad pals that they must listen to the man who had come to bring them a message. Things went better now, and Jim himself was soon made a railroad Y. M. C. A. secretary—a novelty for those days.

With a vision ahead of his time, Scofield saw the need of a building for railroad men where they could write their letters and sit around and take things easy inside decent rooms instead of having to frequent the barrooms for warmth while waiting for their trains. This suggestion was brought before the railroads; they saw the wisdom of it and acted upon it. The result was that a railroad Y. M. C. A. building was put up then and there, and Scofield increasingly won the confidence of the "men of steel."

He continued to visit the sick men and the families of others; and now, when he preached Christ among them, he won souls.

It was in the spring of 1882 that the superintendent of Congregational Home Missions for the Southwest, who had been watching Scofield's work, came to him and told him of a little church that had been organized in Dallas, Texas, and that was going to pieces because it had no minister. Would Scofield give up the practice of law, and go to Texas and take charge of that church?

This was a new proposition indeed! Mr. Scofield prayed about it, and he kept on praying. Some months went by. The Home Missions Superintendent came again and urgently renewed his invitation: the church, he said, was losing the few members it had because of the lack of any pastoral head.

"Yes, I'll go," remarked Scofield emphatically; and as soon as he could arrange his affairs properly he gave up his St. Louis law practice and went straight down to the Dallas church.

IV

DARING TO BE A PASTOR

IT was a midsummer day in 1882, and fearfully hot, when C. I. Scofield reached a little Southwestern town on the bank of a muddy river. It was Dallas, Texas, now the largest city in the State, to which he had gone in obedience to what he believed to be God's call, given him in St. Louis by the Congregational Home Missions Superintendent.

He reached Dallas on a Saturday; and Sunday morning he went to the church building where he was to preach. The people had been notified that he was coming, and a Deacon Page was on hand to meet him at the door. It is not strange that you will see a photograph of Deacon, later Elder, Page framed and on the wall of Dr. Scofield's study to-day.

Counting Deacon Page, there were at the time just twelve members of the First Congregational Church of Dallas; the other eleven were women. Some of the husbands of the women came to some church services, but they were not communicant members. It was not long before practically all of those who came were converted.

The new pastor's first sermon, preached that Sunday morning, was from the text: "The righteous shall flourish like the palm-tree;

he shall grow like a cedar in Lebanon" (Psalm 92:12). He had made a special study of endogenous trees, as a boy, and he took occasion to tell something about the habits and facts of palm-tree life as illuminating the text. (Endogenous plants, like the palm, are the "inside growers," so called: those that grow from within rather than by the addition of layers from without. The believer, with Christ within as his life, grows and flourishes like the palm-tree.)

At the evening service, the same Sunday, he preached from John 3:16: "For God so loved the world, that he gave his only begotten Son, that whosoever believeth in him should not perish, but have everlasting life." He had specially asked the Lord to save some one that night; and the answer to his prayer was two conversions.

Mr. Scofield's Christian service in Y. M. C. A. and other meetings had given him some experience in winning souls to Christ in public meetings. It was his custom to ask, at the close of an evangelistic message, that any present who wished to signify their personal acceptance of Jesus as Saviour would either arise or hold up a hand. Then, at the close of the meeting, he would state that he would be glad to meet all such; he wanted to know them personally; he was sure he had not made everything clear; it was important that they should talk things over together—and the instant the meeting was closed he would be down among the people seeking out those who had given any public expression of their faith, would have them by the hand, and thus, as the other people passed out, he would be in the midst of what proved to be a little after-meeting with the new seekers or converts. This plan was one that God blessed, and it was used in the church at Dallas.

The young preacher was ordained to the Gospel ministry in the Dallas church by a large and representative Council of Congregational ministers and churches. The Council, by a committee of its foremost members, took up, at the insistence of the candidate, the whole question of his past life. He had given but eighteen months to special study for his ordination. Yet those eighteen months of study were so tireless, thorough, and searching, based as they were upon his lifelong habits of study in literature and the law, that very few ministers come up for ordination after studies so unsparing. During this intensive preparation he had studied with profound earnestness and care three standard treatises on systematic theology; had read church history, pastoral theology, and homiletics. Together with all this he had had the extraordinary opportunity of Bible study of an unusual sort under the personal teaching of Dr. James H. Brookes. When he was examined for his ordination, he asked not to be favored in the examination,—and he *was not*. But he was ordained with enthusiastic approval.

Yet in spite of the encouraging beginning in the new church that first Sunday, things went very slowly. There was a bitter prejudice in the South against Congregational churches and ministers. Most Southern people knew the Congregational denomination only as the church of Henry Ward Beecher, the great "Abolitionist," and therefore as a "Yankee church." Little by little the people of Dallas, however, came to learn that the new pastor of the Yankee church was a Confederate soldier. That gave him some social standing, but the people who received him socially would not come near his church, even though they gladly entertained him in their own homes. "Why should he be a Yankee preacher instead of a Presbyterian?" they kept asking.

Well, if the people wouldn't come to hear him, he would go after the people. He capitalized his experience with the St. Louis railroad men, and began persistent visiting in the homes of the folks in Dallas whom he wanted to win. One day, in his church service, he asked if any present would like to have a cottage prayer-meeting in their own home. A twelve-year-old boy raised his hand.

The First Congregational Church in Dallas, Texas. of which
Dr. Scofield was pastor

"Well, what is it?" asked the pastor.

"I think mammy'd like to have yu come," said the boy.

"I'll be there," said the pastor.

At the close of the service he spoke to the boy, and—then or later—he discovered that the boy's father kept one of the lowest barrooms in Dallas. Nothing daunted, Pastor Scofield went to the three-room house on the appointed night. The boy had hustled around and gathered neighbors together in force, probably largely from curiosity. The front room of the little house was packed with people when this unusual "cottage prayer-meeting" began. And the mother and sister of that saloon-keeper's home came to Christ that night. Later the father was saved. That mother is still living; she led probably seventy-five souls to Christ after her conversion.

"Yankee" pastor Scofield made it his custom to hold two such cottage prayer-meetings every week. And people were converted all the time. Such conversions, made in the presence of their neighbors, were genuine. There was no mere "joining the church" formality, as so many people join the church to-day—like a social club. These people took Jesus Christ as their personal Saviour; they knew their neighbors would be watching them to see whether it was going to mean anything in changed lives; they trusted Christ to bring even that miracle to pass; and He was faithful to their trust, as always.

Of course the new converts wanted to connect themselves with Mr. Scofield's church; and they did so. When a new Home Missions Superintendent came to Dallas after six weeks, there were nine to be received into the church, and he was delighted. But he cautioned the new pastor to be careful not to let his church become too much of a *hoi polloi* affair, a "beggars' club." That would never do, he said. As a matter of fact, these humble people who were coming to Christ and joining the First Congregational Church were by no means beggars; they were honest working people. And Mr. Scofield, as he watched the Lord working and trusted the matter wholly to Him, could not help hoping, down in his heart, that the Lord himself, if on earth, would have loved to "join" that church. He would have felt at home there, for so many people there loved Him and had already welcomed Him. So the pastor kept right on taking in as members all who wanted to come, on the basis of personal faith in Jesus Christ as Saviour. Their lives were being revolutionized; and some of them were becoming really prosperous in business and strong citizens.

Two years of this sort of pastoral evangelism had brought the church from a membership of about fourteen to two hundred, and the building was being filled. A young woman of a Michigan family that had moved to Dallas was attending the church, a Miss Hetty Hall van Wart; and about six months after the pastor first met Miss van Wart she became Mrs. Scofield. This was in 1884; and as he and she look back to-day over the thirty-six years since those early beginnings in the Dallas church they praise God together for his goodness in having brought them into each other's lives.

The work of the First Congregational Church went on growing, under God, until a new brick building had to be erected, holding some twelve hundred people; and then two mission churches were planted by the mother church. A large lot adjoining the home church, on a corner, was secured, a big tent was pitched on this for hot summer days, and large evangelistic tent meetings were held, as the blessing of God continued unabated.

Under the preaching of Dr. James H. Brookes, of St. Louis, a boy named W. Irving Carroll had been converted, and had united with Dr. Brookes' church. Not long after that, as he puts it to-day, he "became sadly backslidden and lived a very worldly life for a number of years." Then through the grace of God he was restored to the fellowship of the Lord Jesus Christ, and about this time moved to Dallas. Here he came under the training and Bible teaching of Dr. Scofield, went the whole way with the Lord, and entered the Christian ministry. Then he was made pastor of one of the branches of the home church, the Grand Avenue Congregational Church of Dallas. When Pastor Scofield finally left Dallas, Mr. Carroll was made pastor of the home church itself. And now he is serving as pastor of the famous Washington and Compton Avenues Presbyterian Church of St. Louis, of which Dr. James H. Brookes for years was pastor, and later Dr. Harris H. Gregg.

An illuminating comment on the ministry of the new pastor at Dallas was made in a letter written in 1916 by Mr. W. A. Nason, of Dallas, a member of the church at that time, to Dr. James M. Gray, of the Moody Bible Institute. Mr. Nason wrote:

"When Dr. Scofield came to the church, it was a congregation of confessors and professors; unconverted persons were teaching in the Sunday-school; persons not Christians were employed to sing in the choir. Money was raised in various ways, even to running a dining-hall at the State fair, as other churches of the city were doing. After a while all of this was changed, without direct reference to the inconsistency of the course pursued. In the matter of getting money, some talks were given on the method of raising money among God's children, taking nothing of the Gentiles. Soon it dawned upon us that as God's children we ought to raise the necessary money from Christians to carry on God's work. It was not long before we became self-supporting, and no longer looked to the Home Missionary Society for aid.

"Our members increasing to such an extent that we had to build a new church building, the first act of the finance committee was to pass a resolution to the effect that, as this was to be God's house, we would solicit no funds from an unbeliever, but build

The Deacons and Elders of the First Congregational
Church (Independent) of Dallas, Texas

with money furnished by God's children. We bought the land and erected the building on this basis, and, so far as I know, no money came from an unconverted person.

"The music question was simply settled, not by telling us that it was not right to have unconverted persons singing praises for us to the glory of God, whom they rejected, but by arousing within our hearts the desire to worship God in a way pleasing to Him.

"Our pastor never assumed to be any man's conscience, and, if asked regarding any course of conduct, he would refer to some passage of Scripture and tell the person inquiring to pray for guidance."

The membership of the Dallas church, when finally Pastor Scofield felt led to leave it in order to accept the call to become pastor of Moody's church at Northfield, had risen from its original fourteen members to 551, and 814 members in all had been received. A significant statement occurs in the letter of dismission given to their pastor by the Dallas church: "We commend him to you as one who delights to hide behind the uplifted cross of Jesus; one who will preach a full and free salvation through the shed blood of God's Lamb; one who will lead you into the deep things of the Word, and one who teaches and who preaches the whole truth of God."

Back in St. Louis, immediately after his conversion, Mr. Scofield had first heard and met D. L. Moody. Mr. Moody was at that time holding one of his great evangelistic campaigns in St. Louis; it lasted for five months, and Mr. Scofield had gladly entered into it and had become an active worker in its soul-winning opportunities. The acquaintance thus begun with the great evangelist continued until the latter's death. After becoming pastor of the church in Dallas, Mr. Scofield coveted for his people the blessing of Mr. Moody's testimony and preaching, and twice, at his invitation,

Mr. Moody held series of special meetings in Dallas. The latter's characteristic discernment showed him that Dr. Scofield was a man whom the North and East needed, and, while he was yet an unknown man in the Christian ministry, Mr. Moody invited him to the great Northfield Conference as a speaker. That was his first introduction to the wider fields of acquaintance and service in the Lord's vineyard.

"Moody," says Dr. Scofield to-day, "was one of the greatest men of his generation. I have sometimes thought that Dwight L. Moody and General Grant were, in any true definition of greatness, the greatest men I have ever met. Moody had the strength of his Yankee birth and ancestry; he was a man also of great kindness of heart, with a zeal for souls, and absolutely loyal to the Word of God."

Among the mighty formative influences of Pastor Scofield's life during these years was the far-famed Niagara Bible Conference, held annually at Niagara-on-the-Lake, Ontario. Under Drs. W. J. Erdman, James H. Brookes, Nathaniel West, H. M. Parsons, and others the Bible was taught with the highest scholarly and spiritual power. Dr. Scofield was welcomed into this fellowship and became a favorite teacher.

Invitations to do Bible teaching and preaching at conferences and conventions were coming increasingly to Mr. Scofield while he was at Dallas; and finally, in 1895, it became clear to him that God wanted him to accept the urgent call from Mr. Moody to become pastor of the Congregational Church at East Northfield, Massachusetts, Mr. Moody's own church, and the church home of the students at the great Northfield and Mount Hermon Schools, as well as of the farmers' families permanently living there. When he accepted this pastorate he was also made president of the Northfield Bible Training School. The work gave him an opportunity of

DWIGHT L. MOODY
Foremost Evangelist of his day—Founder of three great schools

preaching to a thousand students every Sunday in addition to his other pastoral opportunities.

For seven years Dr. Scofield ministered at Northfield, during which time Mr. Moody's death occurred. Mr. Carroll, in Dallas, now felt led to give up the pastorate of the First Church there in order to become pastor of the First Presbyterian Church of Texarkana, Texas; and Dr. Scofield was urged to return to his old charge. He consented to do this, returning to Dallas in 1902.

It is interesting to read the following in the action of the ecclesiastical council at Northfield, accepting his resignation:

"The council discern issues of unusual weight in this case. This church gathers and disperses religious forces felt throughout the Union. Each year from all over the country Christian strangers and many from other lands make it a shrine: in part from hallowed associations and more for the pursuit of the higher religious life. The pastor here is, in a measure, a host to Christian pilgrims from half the world. Hence a change of the pastorate touches wide circles in the Gospel kingdom. The pastorate now closing has in its seven years gathered into the church 196 by confession and 112 by letter, a total of 308; and has spent large activities in the yearly convocations held here. It has been marked by strong, skilful, and productive preaching to the dwellers here, to the members of the favored schools here, and to the strangers visiting the town. These have found memorable profit from this pure, fervid, and enriching ministry.

"And while the council can but sympathize with the church for the frequent absences of the pastor to meet the calls which his eminent evangelistic power created, they also rejoice in the blessed gifts which have so profited other churches. We trust the Head of the Church will recompense this Zion by future pastoral faithfulness for the sacrifices thus made for other peoples.

"It is the happiness of the council to record their enjoyment of the personal relations between themselves and Rev. Dr. Scofield. His urbanity, fraternal fulness of heart, and enkindling spiritual fervors have made him a brother beloved by us; and while deploring our loss of these gifts, they give emphasis to our commendation of him to the churches and ministers of Christ to whom he goes."

V

REALLY STUDYING THE BIBLE

IMMEDIATELY after his conversion, in September of 1879, Mr. Scofield had, as has already been pointed out, begun to study the Bible—or he had begun to try to do so. He had speedily realized that he knew almost nothing of the Bible. The saving feature of his ignorance of the Word was that he *knew* that he was ignorant. He inevitably compared his own ignorance and that of most people concerning the Bible with his own thoroughgoing mastery of other things that he had taken up. Naturally a man of that sort could not be content to be a real Christian and have his Bible knowledge of a tenth-rate or even second-rate sort. He must master this as he had been mastering literature, history, and law.

He made various attempts to study the Bible in spots. But he soon discovered that he could not understand the New Testament until he had studied the Old. Indeed, looking back to-day over his lifetime experience in Bible study, he says emphatically that there are not two best ways of studying anything, and there is only one best way to study the Bible: the way it is recorded. The way in which the Holy Spirit decided to record the facts that are brought together in the Bible was, first, by assembling in historical order the books of the Old Testament.

The first verse of the New Testament gave the young convert the clue to proper Bible study. He read there: "The book of the generation of Jesus Christ, the son of David, the son of Abraham." Now, his old-time habit of investigation, dating back to boyhood days, asserted itself. The son of *David*—who was he? The son of *Abraham*—who was he? For that is evidently where the Bible, or the Holy Spirit, begins in recording the life and ministry of the Lord Jesus Christ. Oh, yes, Dr. Scofield knew "something" about Abraham, and he knew "something" about David, as will any one who has been brought up in a Christian family. "That is a part of the 'general knowledge of mankind,' as we lawyers say," said Dr. Scofield in telling of those early Bible-study experiences. This "general knowledge," that is, is such that in the courts you do not have to prove it. But, while the names of David and Abraham were not meaningless to him, he did not know much about them, and he knew that he did not.

When as a boy, stretched out on the floor before the open fire, he became so absorbingly interested in Shakespeare, and biography, and history that, whenever he came across an unknown name, he was driven to read every other book he could lay his hands on to find out more about that unknown name, and then went on to make a boyish but none the less earnest and serious map of universal history, he did not realize that God was preparing him for work in Bible study that was to put the whole Christian world under heavy debt to him as an ambassador of Christ.

This first verse of the first book of the New Testament drove Scofield back to an exhaustive study of David and Abraham. But as he began to dig into what the Bible had to tell about those two characters, he found that, in Bible study, as in everything else, he could not isolate anything; there was nothing to do but to go back and study the whole of the Old Testament. (What the more confirmed him in this was the example of Christ, as given in Luke 24:27, 44.)

And he did. He did not give up studying the New Testament in the meantime,—his soul-winning work compelled its use; but he did not patch up merely bits here and there and call it Bible study, as so many of us do. He went laboriously, thoroughly, painstakingly, tediously on with his work of finding out what God really had to say in His Word. "My method of work, you see," says Dr. Scofield in an apologetic way, "is not what would be called *rapid*; it cannot be made rapid." Come to think of it, just what workers in this world who have put their generations under heavy debt for their life-work, whether in the field of science, or invention, or literature, or art, have been rapid workers! The very idea of rapidity seems to exclude permanent, time-defying results. God is not in a hurry; why should we be?

Not only the first verse of the first chapter of the Gospel of Matthew turned Scofield back to the Old Testament; but such words, spoken of John the Baptist, as "This is he that was spoken of by the prophet Esaias" (Matthew 3:3) also sent him back to the Old Testament for further information. So he must bone down to a personal study of the original sources, and take, not men's opinions, but God's Word.

Not only did his ingrained habits of study force him to treat the Bible in this way, but he felt also that it was only reverent to study the Bible thoroughly. He felt that God's Word deserved it. He felt that there was no excuse for *not* studying the Bible in the most thorough way possible. It is not a big book; he had given far more time already to the study of other books infinitely less worth while, valuable though they had been. Does it not seem strange that these self-evident facts, known in theory to all of us, have not driven more of us to the sort of Bible study which the young converted lawyer felt he must have?

While the beginnings of this new and life-changing study began immediately after his conversion, while he was in St. Louis and still practising law, and while his trusted friend and Bible teacher, Dr. Brookes, guided him and advised his use of certain helpful books, it was not until he gave himself up wholly to Christian work through accepting the pastorate of the church in Dallas that he really got well into his lifetime Bible study. There he began to give his people the results as he dug things out for himself. He preached these results in the pulpit; and he held a regular week-day evening Bible class in his church.

This week-day evening Bible class was not the mid-week prayer-meeting. That he believed should be kept for prayer and testimony; and under his pastorate and guidance his people soon had great liberty in this. In giving their testimonies as to how God had blessed them Pastor Scofield would insist upon their giving a Scripture with every testimony, and they had great blessings from this use of the Scripture.

The Bible-study evenings were open to all who cared to come, and soon people were attending from other churches, and ministers also were coming. Before long a Bible-study class in the Y. M. C. A. was added to the weekly work, and the ministry was extended.

One of the results of the Bible-class work in the Dallas church was the little book, for many years now of world-wide circulation, "Rightly Dividing the Word of Truth." Experience with many students had shown the pastor and Bible teacher that a knowledge of certain truths was essential to any real comprehension of the Bible message. These "beginning truths," as they have been called, were put together by him during his vacation in 1888. The work of making the little book was a time-consuming and laborious task for him then, and "spoiled" his vacation entirely one summer at Niagara. But what a blessing it has been to multitudes of others!

From Dr. Scofield's Personal Bible

It is interesting to run through the fly-leaves of a personal copy of the Bible that Dr. Scofield has used much, and to read some of his notes, and outlines of addresses, and bits of Bible study, and choice quotations. The following are selections from these fly-leaf markings.

1. Repentance	4. Regeneration
2. Faith	5. Adoption
3. Justification	6. Sanctification
	7. Glory

Waiting on the Lord

1. Psalm 62 : 1 "silent"
2. Psalm 104 : 27 "depend upon — wait expectantly"
3. 2 Chron. 7 : 18, 19 { To wait as a servant
   Prov. 8 : 34 { or soldier

To wait upon God is to be silent that he may speak; expecting all things from him; and girt for instant unquestioning obedience to the slightest movement of his will.
Illust. 2 Sam. 23 : 13-17
1. They were separated unto David
2. They were near
3. They were silent
4. David's sigh was their command

"One may have an intelligent opinion about divine things, and be a worthy man; but the **taste** of divine things, the **realizing sense** of what they are, belongs only to those in whom the Spirit lives ungrieved." —Jonathan Edwards.

There are some who desire to know with the sole purpose that they may know, and it is base curiosity; and some who desire to know that they may be known, and it is base ambition; and some who desire to know that they may sell their knowledge for wealth and honor, and it is base avarice; but there are some, also, who desire to know that they may be edified, and it is prudence; and some who desire to know that they may help others, and it is charity.—Bernard.

Rom. 4. The Blessed Man

"All".

Leave all	Luke 5 : 11
Believe all	Luke 24 : 25
Obey all	Matt. 28 : 20; Acts 5 : 29
Receive all	1 Cor. 3 : 22, John 20 : 22, Matt. 28 : 18
Go to all	Matt. 28 : 19

Burning Quest. our day
Insp. and Auth. the O. T.
For 30 years Higher Criticism
— Pentateuch — composite — not Mosaic
— Deut. especially late forgery
— Historical Books full errors
— No Psalm by David
— No predictive element in Proph.
— Daniel a forgery

The words "one" and "once" in the following verses are underlined and connected Hebrews 10 . 2, 10, 12, and 14.

" I paused last eve beside the blacksmith's
     door,
   And heard the anvil ring the vespers
     chime,
   And looking in, I saw upon the floor
   Old hammers worn with beating years of
     time.

" 'How many anvils have you had,' said I,
   'To wear and batter all these hammers
     so?'
   'Just one,' he answered. Then, with twin-
     kling eye,
   'The anvil wears the hammers out, you
     know.'

" And so I thought, the anvil of God's Word
   For ages skeptics' blows have beat upon,
   But though the noise of falling blows was
     heard,
   The anvil is unchanged, the hammer
     gone."

Brethren in the Dallas church furnished money for composition and plates for a first edition of the book, and shortly after this the well-known New York publishers of sound Bible literature, Loizeaux Brothers, purchased the plates and publishing rights, and have continued the publication of the book until this day. They have brought out some thirty-seven different editions, and other editions have been issued by other publishers. Doubtless hundreds of thousands of copies of the book have thus gone into circulation, and its mission of blessing still continues.

Among the more important of the by-products of the Dallas work must be mentioned the formation and training of a class of young men obviously having pastoral and evangelistic gifts. While many participated in the instruction in part, ten such students continued through the course and, having made full proof of their spiritual gifts in many searching experiences, received ordination. It is gratifying to record that the seal of the Divine blessing has been wonderful upon the varied ministry of these men.

For fifteen years Mr. Scofield went patiently, studiously, comprehensively on in his thorough-going Bible study, mastering what he set out to do, as he hunted down through the pages of the Word of God the precious facts and truths that he was after, and that the Holy Spirit opened up and illuminated to him. Using the results of his work as he did for his constant teaching and preaching, he was keeping them also carefully written out in full notes, preserving them systematically. These studies were later, and little by little, embodied in what finally became the Scofield Bible Correspondence Course. This Course had begun by the issuing of pamphlets, covering portions of the Word, until the time came when it was possible to bring such pamphlets together in the three Bible Correspondence Course volumes which have been used by such great numbers, and which are to-day a permanent and rich contribution to the Bible study of the English-speaking Christian world, as ministered by the Moody Bible Institute.

It was when Dr. Scofield accepted Mr. Moody's invitation to become pastor of the Congregational church at Northfield (1895–1902) that the Correspondence Course was completed. Even then it was gone over again, and revised, references were verified, and the whole was made more thorough and complete.

Into it had gone fifteen years of unremitting study of the Bible. And by "study" is not meant the reading of a number of books of an expository and exegetical nature, together with critical works. That also was done; but the foundation of it all was *study of the Word itself*. Oh, those days and nights of toil! And ever the rubbish heap grew—a stack for the sake of tracing out a single line some-times—nay, sometimes a single word. People to whom the Scofield Correspondence Course or the Reference Bible notes may seem very simple and easy do not realize that a vast amount of investigation and research went into deciding what *not* to put into annotations. The *attainment* of truth, the *interrelation* of truth, the finding—few can know at what cost of toil—the simplest, clearest word for the *expression* of truth: all this was part of the costliness of the study. And all this as a preparation, though the toiler knew it not, for the making, years later, of the Reference Bible.

About ten thousand different students, from practically every country on earth and the islands of the sea, studied the Correspondence Course while Dr. Scofield was personally in charge of it. This great number represented almost every walk in life. Many ministers wrote to Dr. Scofield that the Correspondence Course had transformed their ministry. One such minister said that he had studied Hebrew and Greek in his seminary in order to be able to study the Bible in the original. But, like so many others, having thus learned the Hebrew and the Greek, his Bible study stopped right there—rather, it never began. For he never studied the *Bible* until he came into touch with the Scofield Correspondence Course: and then for the first time he learned by experience what real study of God's Word was.

Dr. Scofield kept up the personal direction of the Correspondence School work from 1890 to 1915. It having then become necessary for him to commit this laborious work to other hands, the Correspondence Department of the Moody Bible Institute made arrangements with him to take it over; and any lover of the Bible, or one who wants to become an intelligent lover and student of the Bible, can now have access to the results of those years of painstaking study by taking the course through the Moody Bible Institute.[1]*

---

1 * Information concerning this Course may be had by addressing the Moody Bible Institute, 153 Institute Place, Chicago.

VI

VICTORY AND MISSIONS

ALTHOUGH God had greatly blessed the Dallas pastor in his own life, and was blessing his studies in the Word to himself and to others, he had not yet entered into the New Testament teaching of the life of power and victory. There were times when he was anxious; he knew this was unnecessary and wrong, and he longed to step out fully into the normal New Testament Christian experience. It was in harmony with his method of patient thoroughness in all his studies that he finally apprehended the truth as related to the new life in Christ Jesus.

The Southwest, in the years of Scofield's first ministry in Dallas, seethed with so-called holiness testimony. Probably no phase of the various teachings on the holy life was unrepresented. To all of it in those beginning-days of his Christian life and service he lent an eager ear—eager because of an intense desire to realize in his own experience the highest Christian life. But of necessity he must bring those methods, to the results of which he was hearing rapturous testimonies, to the test of Scripture. Again and again he was compelled to turn from the theories which he was hearing. Not so spoke the Word.

The light broke in through a study of the threefold experience of the Apostle Paul. Beginning as a self-satisfied, self-righteous legalist, Paul met Jesus on the Damascus road and became a justified man; but still a man under the defeats recorded in the seventh of Romans. Passing then into the marvellous victories of the eighth of Romans, it was plain that Paul ascribed these victories (Romans 8:2) to the new life in Christ Jesus as energized and made effectual through the indwelling Holy Spirit. The eager seeker found that great triumph chapter athrill with the Spirit. Passing over the parenthetic ninth, tenth, and eleventh chapters to the twelfth—the true continuation of the eighth—he found the disclosure of the step into victory—and not victory over the Adamic self merely, but into the whole life of fruitful service and fulness of joy. The new act of faith demanded the presentation (or yielding) of the body, demanded not only the cessation of conscious resistance to Christ, but also the acceptance of the Christ life plan as one of sacrifice. A life no longer to serve self, but Christ. The thing demanded was an act as definite as the act of faith in which the new life began.

When this was perceived, the answer in Scofield's soul was obedience. From that moment a new experience of fruitful service and of inner blessing began.

And now, when he had entered into the whole blessing, he found to his delight that he had long before been getting blessed glimpses of this New Testament truth through his study of the Old Testament types. He saw that the Jehovah Jesus foretold and foreshadowed throughout the entire Law and the Prophets had provided for him not only salvation from the penalty of sin, but also salvation from its power and all-sufficiency for peace and joy and the ninefold fruit of the Spirit (Galatians 5:22, 23).

At the Niagara Bible Conference Pastor Scofield met, for several successive years, Hudson Taylor, the founder and director of the China Inland Mission. Through Mr. Taylor he began to have an interest in foreign missions. This set him to studying the Bible to get God's direct word on that subject. He saw that the China Inland Mission was wonderfully apostolic in its spirit, plan, and purposes, and he had the rare privilege of many talks with Mr. Taylor.

About this time he came across a book by the brilliant journalist-traveler, William Eleroy Curtis, who had been sent by the United States Government, before the opening of the World's Fair in Chicago in 1893, to South and Central America in order to stir up an interest there in the coming exposition. Scofield read with deepest interest what Mr. Curtis had to say about the great lands to our south. He had an opportunity of hearing Mr. Curtis speak, and he was impressed when the speaker told of the religious destitution of Central America, containing nearly three million souls, yet with only dissolute priests making a mockery of ministering to them spiritually. The only Protestant missionary in Central America apparently was at Guatemala, while the Moravian brethren had a mission on the coast.

Now Scofield made a careful study of the Bible plan of evangelizing the world—which he still believes to be the only true plan. He found there that the early Christians, acting under the direct instruction of our Lord Jesus Himself, began their evangelizing in Jerusalem, went on into all Judea, then to Samaria, and then on progressively "unto the uttermost part of the earth" (Acts 1:8). Evidently it was God's purpose that Christians should evangelize *as they go*, not overleaping great sections of the earth in telling mankind the good news of Jesus.

So, "beginning at Dallas," the question arose: What is the *nearest* unevangelized section to *me?* The answer seemed to be Mexico. But upon investigation Scofield found that there were seven strong denominations working in Mexico. That could not be said to be wholly neglected. Pushing on still farther, what was the next possible section? Central America. He believed that the Lord had called his attention to Central America through the writing and speaking of Curtis. But before entering upon any missionary enterprise there, Scofield wrote to different denominational mission boards and asked whether they would be willing to undertake the evangelizing of Central America. Without exception these boards answered that they were already staggering under heavy burdens in their missionary work and obligations, and could not conscientiously enter a new field. It was only then that he felt clear that God was calling him to this unoccupied region.

The mission-aroused pastor now called together for special prayer three of the consecrated men of his church, men who knew how to pray, and who had given their lives utterly to the Lord—E. M. Powell, Luther Rees, and W. A. Nason. The little group of pastor and laymen earnestly asked the Lord to use them to evangelize Central America.

After they had prayed about the matter, the subject was brought before the entire church, and there it was taken up with prayers and literally with tears. Missionary volunteers began to offer for the field. And from that time the Dallas church began to spend more money on missions than on home expenses, and has kept this up ever since.

That was the beginning of the now well-established and greatly blessed Central American Mission. It was formed at the home of the pastor, in Dallas, on November 14, 1890. Dr. Scofield was made secretary, Mr. Powell the treasurer, and Mr. Rees the chairman, of the Council. In 1893 the Hon. D. H. Scott, of Paris, Texas, was added to the Council, and in 1894 he became Treasurer of the Mission, continuing in that office ever since. From the start it has been a faith mission, depending upon God and not upon men or organizations. The services of the Council are wholly gratuitous—no rent—the only items of expense being postage and printing, and these largely met by the subscriptions to the Bulletin, which is now issued bi-monthly.

The statement of belief of the Central American Mission is interesting and significant: "We believe in one God, revealed as existing in three equal persons, Father, Son, and Holy Spirit; in the death of Jesus Christ for our sins as a true substitute; in salvation by faith alone without works; in good works as the fruit of salvation; in the Scriptures of the Old and New Testaments as verbally inspired in the original writings; and in a future state of unending blessedness for the saved and unending conscious suffering for the lost."

As to other details, the Mission is conducted on the following basis: "The Mission is *interdenominational*. It does not seek to reproduce on mission grounds the divisions of Protestantism: *Evangelical*—it holds to the faith once for all delivered to the saints. **Evangelistic**—it believes that the evangelization of the world, not its civilization, is the true work of the church. Two other principles are fundamental: The Mission does not *personally solicit* either missionaries or money, and *no salaries* are paid to any one."

During the thirty years since its beginning, the needs of the Mission and its missionaries have always been met. Never once has there been a failure. There are now ninety-two churches in the field of Central America, with about five thousand five hundred members, as the result of this work. From the Dallas church alone some nine missionaries have gone to Central America, and a number from the same church to other foreign fields.

The bi-monthly Bulletin of the Central American Mission is interesting reading to-day. (It is published at Paris, Texas, at the very nominal subscription price of twenty-five cents a year; those who would have fellowship in the work of this Mission will do well to secure its regular visits in their homes.)

Perhaps readers of this Life Story would like to put in thei prayer-lists the names of the missionaries of this Mission that wa born in faith and prayer, and ask God to go on in ever-increasing blessing through them to the needy field so near home. The mission aries are as follows:

A. E. Bishop, Box 74, Guatemala City, Guatemala.

Mrs. A. E. Bishop, Box 74, Guatemala City, Guatemala.

Mrs. Caspar Wistar, Box 74, Guatemala City, Guatemala.

Miss A. F. Houser, Box 74, Guatemala City, Guatemala.

Miss B. E. Zimmerman, Box 74, Guatemala City, Guatemala.

Dr. H. A. Becker, Box 74, Guatemala City, Guatemala.

Mrs. H. A. Becker, Box 74, Guatemala City, Guatemala.

A. B. Treichler, Solola, Guatemala.

Mrs. A. B. Treichler, Solola, Guatemala.

F. G. Toms, Huehuetenango, Guatemala.

Mrs. F. G. Toms, Huehuetenango, Guatemala.

H. W. Toms, Huehuetenango, Guatemala.

Mrs. H. W. Toms, Huehuetenango, Guatemala.

Mrs. Rosemma V. B. Hunter, Escuintla, Guatemala.

J. T. Butler, Zacapa, Guatemala.

Mrs. J. T. Butler, Zacapa, Guatemala.

W. C. Townsend, Antigua, Guatemala.

Mrs. W. C. Townsend, Antigua, Guatemala.

Mrs. F. W. Boyle, Box 289, San Jose, Costa Rica.

Miss A. G. McLean, Box 289, San Jose, Costa Rica.

W. H. Hooper, Box 36, Managua, Nicaragua.

Mrs. W. H. Hooper, Box 36, Managua, Nicaragua.

Miss Annie E. Thomas, Box 36, Managua, Nicaragua.

Karl D. Hummel, Box 36, Managua, Nicaragua.

Mrs. Karl D. Hummel, Box 36, Managua, Nicaragua.

L. W. McConnell, Box 149, San Salvador, Salvador.

Mrs. L. W. McConnell, Box 149, San Salvador, Salvador.

Mrs. Gertrude Bell, Box 149, San Salvador, Salvador.

I. S. Smith, Cojutepeque, Salvador.

Mrs. I. S. Smith, Cojutepeque, Salvador.

Miss Laura Nelson, Dulce Nombre de Copan, Honduras.

W. F. Aberle, Santa Rosa de Copan, Honduras.

Mrs. W. F. Aberle, Santa Rosa de Copan, Honduras.

Miss Beatrice Newman, Santa Rosa de Copan, Honduras.

C. F. Lincoln, Comayaguela, Tegucigalpa, Honduras.

Mrs. C. F. Lincoln, Comayaguela, Tegucigalpa, Honduras.

Miss Marion Steinbach, Comayaguela, Tegucigalpa, Honduras.

Herbert R. Peaslee, Choluteca, Honduras.

Miss A. J. Gohrman, Colinas, Santa Barbara, Honduras.

VII

THE REFERENCE BIBLE BEGUN

A BOUT the year 1902 Dr. Scofield was one day talking to a very dear friend in New York City—a layman and business man, Mr. Alwyn Ball, whose sympathetic friendship and co-operation had meant much to him in his work. "Dr. Scofield," said Mr. Ball, "just what work are you now looking ahead to or planning, beyond the Bible conference teaching work that you constantly do, and in addition to your Bible Correspondence Course? What Bible work have you in mind that will remain permanently after you are gone?"

Challenged by this question, Dr. Scofield told his friend something of what had been running through his mind as to the need of a Reference Bible that should be helpful to those who wanted to do systematic Bible study for themselves, yet without being too formidable in size and annotations. Mr. Ball at once said that he believed the Lord wanted Dr. Scofield to bring out such a work. And with that conversation there came the conviction from God, clearly revealed to the pastor and Bible student, that the Lord indeed wanted him to undertake this. From that time on he never doubted God's call to the vast undertaking. Soon afterward the late John C. Pirie, of Chicago and New York, entered heartily into fellowship with Dr. Scofield in the very considerable expense involved in the work.

Through his ministry in teaching Bible classes of ordinary men and women, his Bible Correspondence Course work reaching great numbers of such people, and his simple but searching and fundamental studies in the little book, "Rightly Dividing the Word of Truth," Dr. Scofield had had abundant evidence that multitudes of persons everywhere were needing and hungering for just such guidance in their Bible study as he had been providentially led to discover for himself and to give to others. But the time had come when he saw that if his Bible studies were to be of the widest usefulness they would need to be attached to the Word itself—and in a form not too bulky. Out of his own past experience he asked himself the question: "What kind of reference Bible would have helped me most when I was first trying to learn something of the Word, but ignorant of the very first principles of Bible study?" Looking back then over twenty years of such study, and visualizing again his own need as an uninstructed beginner when he had first come to Christ, he began to see the sort of reference Bible that would have been most useful to him, and that he believed was still greatly needed.

After serving seven years as pastor of the church in East Northfield at Mr. Moody's call, Dr. Scofield, as will be remembered, had returned to his old charge in Dallas, Texas, in 1902. The people of the Dallas church now assured him that they would be content to have him give his time freely to work on the proposed Reference Bible if he would continue to serve them as their pastor. This was the joint work that he undertook to do; but after a year of it, in 1903, he found that he would either have to give his entire time to work on the Reference Bible or give it up—and he dared not do *that*. So the church, in unselfish devotion to the largest service of their Lord and Master, set him free to give uninterrupted attention to the Bible work, though his name was continued as their pastor until 1907, when he became pastor emeritus.

And now seven years (from 1902 until the work was published in 1909) were given to a complete re-study of the Bible, a task that would have been impossible within that time had not the ground been so thoroughly covered in preparing the Correspondence Course.

Dr. Scofield saw clearly that what was needed was not a commentary on the Bible, but the Bible itself with just enough help in reference form to keep the reader and student close to the Word of God. As he studied and pondered this, very early in his new work the entire plan of what is now the Scofield Reference Bible came to him. Few details were changed or added afterward.

He saw, for example, the immense value of a system of chain references which should cover, one by one, all the great subjects or teachings of the Bible, commencing with the first clear mention of such a subject or theme in the Bible, and then continuing from passage to passage of every outstanding mention until the last such mention in the Bible was reached. At the place of final mention the series of references would be concluded by a clear, compact note summarizing the entire teaching of the Bible on that theme. The value of this simple help to Bible study, for one who wishes to find out for himself what God says on any of these subjects, is immense. It needs only to be stated to have its rare helpfulness clearly seen.

Each book of the Bible must have a simple, clear introduction, and must also be accompanied by a brief analysis of the book.

Then there must be an introduction to each group of books, such as the Pentateuch, the Historical Books, the Poetical Books, the Prophetical Books, and the rest.

He felt that a system of paragraphing, not following exactly any paragraphed Bible—though there were many of these—but breaking up the material into paragraphs at such points as the narrative or message seemed best to warrant, and each paragraph to be headed by a clear sub-title which would give the reader an instant suggestion of the contents of that paragraph, would help to guide the student's thought in the right channel. This feature of the Reference Bible has been warmly approved, especially by ministers, who have found sermonic help in these sub-heads. Dr. Scofield has owned his indebtedness to Dr. R. A. Torrey for the suggestion of this feature.

Just here one of the secrets of the world-wide usefulness of the Scofield Reference Bible should be disclosed. How is it that ministers and Bible teachers, of advanced scholarship and mature learning in Bible fields, as well as the ordinary untaught lay reader of the Bible, alike find this work of untold value? How is it that seminary professors and leading Bible students and ministers of directly opposed views in Bible interpretation and in theological positions alike find this Bible of greatest use to them?

For example, a very prominent Arminian theologian and a very prominent Calvinist theologian almost at the same time told Dr. Scofield that they had been examining with much interest his definitions of crucial doctrinal words, such as Election, Predestination, and Foreordination. And both of these men said to him, in effect, that they found that they could accept his definitions. One or the other said, to be sure, that he might guard this point or that a little in his own statement of the doctrine; he might phrase this or that point a little differently; but that, on the whole, he found the definitions in the Scofield Reference Bible sound and satisfactory.

How can this be explained? The answer is simple. The man who gave his lifetime study to the making of the notes and comments in the Scofield Reference Bible was concerned only to *find and state exactly what the Bible itself had to say* on any and every point. And not every one recognizes that the *Bible* is a book on which all true believers can stand, if we are satisfied to have Biblical instead of philosophical or theological definitions. It is the undiluted Scripture basis of its notes and comments that makes the Scofield Reference Bible so invaluable and so almost unique.

Look, for example, at the definition of Predestination, which is given in a foot-note on Ephesians 1:5: "Having predestinated us unto the adoption of children by Jesus Christ to himself, according to the good pleasure of his will." Here is the definition: "Predestination is that effective exercise of the will of God by which things before determined by Him are brought to pass."

Now a good many people think, and naturally enough from the mere meaning of the word "predestination" itself, that this word means the determining by God, in advance, of what is to be brought to pass. But God does not say so. He says, in His Word, that predestination is that exercise of His will by which He brings to pass those things which, earlier, He had determined. On this the Word of God is unmistakable; therefore, for believers, that is final. If one still is skeptical as to this, he has but to search out for himself exactly what God says about predestination, by using the chain references to this which are brought together for his quick finding in the margins of the Reference Bible.

Or notice the definition of Election as given in a note in comment on 1 Peter 1:2: "Elect according to the foreknowledge of God the Father." After a statement on the meanings of the Hebrew and Greek words in both Testaments rendered "elect," "chosen," etc., comes this brief, clean-cut, summarizing definition: "Election is, therefore: (1) The sovereign act of God in grace whereby certain are chosen from among mankind for Himself (John 15:19). (2) The sovereign act of God whereby certain elect persons are chosen for distinctive service for Him (Luke 6:13; Acts 9:15; 1 Corinthians 1:27, 28)."

Of course we must, as Dr. Scofield points out, be willing to leave out the *lacunæ*, the intentional gaps in the Bible, the things left unsaid by God, and not attempt to form opinions or draw inferences as to those silences. "*Don't infer doctrines in your Bible study*," is one of the cardinal principles upon which Dr. Scofield has long worked and which he urges upon other Bible students. What does *God say?*—that is what you must find out. When God does not say anything on a certain subject, then leave it alone.

For example, in studying the relation of God's foreknowledge to His predestination, the question naturally arises, as we follow the points back step by step, *What* does God "foreknow"? But the Bible gives us no light on this. Therefore the only safe answer is, "I don't know." We must leave what constitutes God's foreknowledge to Him, for He has not told us.

The brief, easily read definitions now found in the Reference Bible did not come easily. First of all, there were constant prayer and seeking of divine guidance; an utter yet confident dependence upon the illumination of God's Spirit. Then there was an enormous amount of study, the leaving of no stone unturned in order to make sure of finding just what God has put there for us to find if we are willing to search. All this meant that often an incredible amount of time, and energy, and patient study, and faith-filled prayer went into the formation of some little two-line definition.

But the editor of the Scofield Reference Bible was too reverent and too thorough to imagine that he alone had been taught of the Spirit, and this recognition of other scholarly and spiritual students involved the additional immense labor of the study of their writings. The result is that those definitions last, and they satisfy, and God can bless them, as He is doing, to multitudes of his children.

The problem of what to put into the Reference Bible, in the way of notes and comments, and what to leave out, was solved by prayer, as only it could be. But in addition to the supernatural illumination of the Holy Spirit, God was capitalizing the rich experience that pastor Scofield had had during his years of teaching the Bible in his Dallas pastorate. Those years of experience had shown him that there are certain places in Bible study where many students and readers of the Bible become confused or are misled. On these passages, therefore, he knew that some comment was needed, and he acted accordingly, while at the same time using constant care not to let the Reference Bible become a mere commentary.

The spiritual value of the Scofield Reference Bible has been well brought out by Dr. James M. Gray, of the Moody Bible Institute, in a characterization of Dr. Scofield's distinctive gifts. Dr. Gray has said:

"The Scofield Reference Bible requires no more advertising than the juicy grass requires to draw the hungry sheep....

"When one attempts to describe Dr. Scofield in the pulpit or the teacher's desk, that open-air meeting in Jerusalem comes into mind where 'they read in the book of the law of God distinctly, and gave the sense, and caused them to understand the reading' (Nehemiah 8:8).

"This is Dr. Scofield's richest gift. He knows how to read the Word of God, and give the sense, and cause the people to understand the reading. He never writes or speaks in a haze. As was said of another, 'No trace of indeterminateness can be found in any of his discussions on any subject.' His insight pierces the intricacies.

"A Christian father, himself charmed by the Scofield Reference Bible, was pleased to see his young sons take it up night after night because, they said, 'it was so easy to find out things.' Thank God for a Bible expositor who can command the interest of children!

"One of the officials of the Oxford University Press wrote me that in reading proof for another printing of that book he 'found it almost impossible to concentrate on the technical work because of the temptation to follow the great Bible truths so delightfully unfolded and connected by Dr. Scofield's genius.' And yet it was not Dr. Scofield's genius so much that did the work, but the 'unction of the Holy One' that came upon him for the service....

"When our beloved brother was revising his Correspondence Course he honored me with advance sheets and with the request that I go over his definitions of the great words of Scripture for any suggestions that might occur to me. It was like a considerate father giving his lad the end of the reins to hold and letting him think he was driving the horse.

"In the quiet of my study the work was done. No eye but that of God rested upon me; and as I followed in the definitions the unveiling of the Bible meaning of such words as 'adoption' and 'atonement,' and 'redemption' and 'remission,' and 'pardon' and 'peace,' I am glad to be able to say that my heart swelled within me and that my emotions found outlet in the falling tear. A teacher who can accomplish that in one can never be forgotten....

"Dr. Scofield sees the inner truth and hidden glories of the Holy Scriptures as few Christian teachers do. To him the Bible from beginning to end is luminous with the splendors of Christ. And as his clear analysis and sublime logic unveil those splendors, his own joy and ecstasy in them become contagious."

It is not strange that this Reference Bible has been called for by missionaries in foreign fields, with its notes and comments and references and paragraph headings translated into the languages in which the missionaries are working. Requests for permission to translate have come from many if not all of the larger mission fields. It is not known to Dr. Scofield or to the biographer just what translations exist, except that he has been told from time to time that these have been made in various languages. Meantime the English editions are carrying their blessing to missionaries the world over, and through them to both saved and unsaved of many tongues.

VIII

DRUDGERY AND GENIUS

EALIZING that he could never give himself as he should to the making of the new Reference Bible except by withdrawing from every other form of service, Dr. and Mrs. Scofield went abroad in 1904 to take up this work. Both were very weary, and Mrs. Scofield had never seen London, so they went there first, with no special purpose in mind except a bit of sight-seeing. At this time Dr. Scofield had no plans as to a publisher for the Reference Bible. He had not even thought of that important detail in the work, not appreciating then, as he has since, how vitally important it was that the right publisher should be found.

In Northfield he had become well acquainted with the older Mr. Scott of the well-known firm of religious publishers in London, Morgan & Scott. He welcomed the Scofields to London, and took them with him for a little visit at his country place at Dorking. There Dr. Scofield told Mr. Scott quite fully about the work he had undertaken in planning a new Reference Bible.

"Who is going to publish it?" at once asked Mr. Scott.

"I do not know," was the reply. "I have not taken that up. The first thing I must do is to get the material ready; then it will be time enough to think of a publisher."

"But the question of the publisher is of the utmost importance," replied Mr. Scott. "And there is only one concern that ought to publish that Bible. My own house would be glad to publish it, of course; but we could not give it the world-wide introduction which it must have. The publishers of this Bible must be the Oxford University Press."

"I do not know any one connected with the Oxford Press," said Dr. Scofield.

"I can easily arrange that," answered Mr. Scott; and forthwith he took his friend to call upon Mr. Henry Frowde, then the head of the great Bible publishing house of Great Britain and the English-speaking world.

Mr. Frowde was interested. He said he would consult Mr. Armstrong, then head of the American branch of the Oxford University Press. Mr. Armstrong was immediately enthusiastic at the suggestion that this new Reference Bible be brought out by the Oxford Press, and a preliminary understanding was quickly reached. Mr. Frowde assured Dr. Scofield that, if he finally decided to place the Bible with them, they could readily arrange a proper contract for the publication, in the interests of each party. And so the publishing question was settled, God having fulfilled his word that "before they call, I will answer" (Isaiah 65:24).

Dr. and Mrs. Scofield now went from London to Montreux, Switzerland, for quiet work and study. Here he fell desperately ill. It was evidently one of the several attacks that Satan began making upon him and this work of putting the riches of God's Word freely at the disposal of multitudes who otherwise would not have them. The story of the Adversary's persistent, desperate, but futile attempts to prevent the successful completion of the Scofield Reference Bible is a significant and impressive one. Satan is a terrible adversary; but, praise God, he is an "already defeated foe."

For three or four months Dr. Scofield's illness prevented his doing anything further. Before this illness began he had given an order in Geneva for the making of several big blank books, one for each of the grand divisions of the Bible, such as the Pentateuch, the Historical Books, the Poetical Books, the Prophetical Books, and the rest. These books consisted of large blank pages, and his plan was to paste the text of the Scriptures from a good edition of the Bible on these blank pages, then make his references and annotations and comments on the margins. For the Bible text for this use the Oxford Press had given him half a dozen copies of their most accurate edition, of which the proof had been read thirteen different times.

While he lay sick and helpless, utterly incapacitated for going on with his work, Mrs. Scofield, unknown to him, pasted up the entire Bible in the big blank books that had come from Geneva. Upon his recovery he found this preliminary part of the work finished, and the books ready for him to go ahead. Broad four-inch margins on all four sides of the Bible text on each page of the books gave ample room for the necessary editorial work. This was but the beginning of the large contributions made by his devoted wife to the monumental work that lay ahead for both of them.

Worn out from his illness, Scofield was far from strong when he now settled down to the real work for which he had been unconsciously collecting material during the twenty-five years since his conversion, and even earlier. But the Lord was his strength, and was going to complete that which He had begun.

In making the chain references, which were to be one of the central features of the new Bible, the very first mention of every great theme or subject had first to be located; then patiently all the other most important references to the same theme throughout the entire Bible, Old Testament and New, must be searched out and brought together. Each theme or subject was searched out, carried through the entire Bible, and completed before another theme or subject was taken up. All this involved a concentration and continuance and infinite painstaking in detail of labor that probably no one can imagine who has not done some such work. "May the Lord spare you that kind of work," said Dr. Scofield fervently to a friend years afterward.

These chain references were not written into the margins of the big books at first; they were carefully brought together and written out by the compiler and editor on separate sheets of paper; and then they were transferred from those sheets into the big books themselves. And fully half of this work of entering them finally into the books was done by Mrs. Scofield.

The conscious purpose that Dr. Scofield had in doing this work comes out in his characteristic statement: "If you're going to *do* it, and do it for God, there is only one way—not a smooth, easy way, but *as unto the Lord.*"

For example, he found that in making accurate and illuminating subheads for the paragraphs of the Reference Bible in the Gospels, there must be a careful study of all the parallel passages before any subhead could be safely decided upon for any paragraph in any one Gospel. Parallel passages bearing on that paragraph in another Gospel might alone determine the correct subhead. This patient sort of search and painstaking comparing Scripture with Scripture characterized the making of the Reference Bible at every point. This it was that prevented rapid work, that added almost incalculably to the labor, and that enabled God to bless the work as He has done.

On that first foreign trip for the making of the Reference Bible the introductions to the larger or grand divisions of the books of the Bible were written, the introductions to each of the sixty-six

GRAY SHINGLES
DOUGLASTON ROAD
DOUGLASTON, LONG ISLAND, NY

10 Nov/15—

Oxford Univ. Press.
35 W. 32nd St.
N.Y. City.

Dear Mr. McIntosh.

Please change "God" in Genesis
G. 5, Scofield Ref. Bible, to GOD (i.e. indicating
that Jehovah is meant.

Yours very sincerely
C. I. Scofield

books, and the analyses of each of the sixty-six books. This first retirement abroad in order to give undivided attention to the work lasted for eleven months, nine of which were spent in solid work at Montreux.

About this time the First Congregational Church in Dallas was having a difficult time, becoming somewhat disheartened on account of the long absence of the one who was nominally its pastor, though it had been clearly understood that he must be free to give his whole time to this work; and the people of the church urged Dr. Scofield to return and let them have a little of his time, assuring him that he would still be free to go on with his labors on the Bible. At the same time the problem of the providing of money for the continuing of his sojourn abroad had arisen. He says frankly to-day, in looking back at that particular time in his work, that he suffered a weakening of his faith as to God's purpose to provide the money and see him through this tremendous task. And so he came back to America, and took up preaching and pastoral work in Dallas. The Lord had, indeed, provided all the money needs hitherto—even when "the bottom of the barrel" had more than once just about been reached, the Lord's provision always arrived before there was any real suffering.

It was not long after resuming preaching and pastoral work at Dallas that Dr. Scofield realized that it was impossible to attempt to go on with his Bible work and church work together. He had somewhat of a breakdown in health again. This time he spent a winter at the Sanitarium at Clifton Springs, New York,—not so much as an invalid as because of the splendid facilities there for the best food and air, and medical attention when needed, and at the same time freedom to go on with his work.

He took up quarters there that gave him every facility for working, and with Miss Ella E. Pohle, who had done invaluable secretarial work for him for years in connection with the Bible Correspondence Course, he again entered upon the arduous labors of the Reference Bible. Mrs. Scofield and Miss Pohle worked together in putting the multitudinous chain references into place on the pages of the big books that were gradually constituting "copy" for the final work, after Dr. Scofield had carefully prepared these references himself on separate sheets.

It must be remembered that every entry of a reference in this chain reference plan required three separate lines. First came the topic or theme, such as "Gospel" or "Inspiration." Then came the chapter and verse reference for the next succeeding passage of Scripture where that same topic or theme occurred. Finally came, in parentheses, the references for the first mention of that topic or theme in Scripture, and its last mention. For example, on the passage in 2 Kings 6:6, where Elisha makes the axe-head to swim, you will find the chain reference entry in the margin: "Miracles (Old Testament), verses 5–7, 18–20; 2 Kings 13:21. (Genesis 5:24; Jonah 2:1–10)."

Now multiply this work for each entry by the number of such entries you find in the Old Testament and the New in the Scofield Reference Bible, recalling that each such entry was written out first at least twice by Dr. Scofield himself, and then by those who were helping him to transfer the references to the final "copy" for the printer, and you begin to have a hint of what this task involved. And that was only one detail in the great work.

IX

THE DEBT TO SCHOLARSHIP

A FTER a winter at Clifton Springs it became clear to Dr. and Mrs. Scofield that they should go to Europe again. This time Oxford was the destination; and a two years' stay in that wonderful English university town followed. Here the treasures of the Oxford libraries were fully at the disposal of the man who was making himself a Bible scholar by mastering the Bible scholarship of the world. He was by no means content to limit his studies and researches to constructive and believing Bible scholarship. He covered the whole field of such scholarship, whether friendly or unfriendly to the Bible. He wanted to know at first-hand all that the critics claimed to have done, and he was open to any light that their scholarly researches might, known or unknown to themselves, throw upon the Word of God. He found Prof. Dr. William Sanday, an outstanding scholarly critic, gracious in his readiness to confer. So also with the more extreme critic, Prof. S. R. Driver. Of the conservative Bible scholars abroad, Dr. Scofield gratefully acknowledges his indebtedness to Profs. A. H. Sayce and David Samuel Margoliouth, of Oxford, and to Mr. Walter Scott, the eminent Bible teacher.

It was Dr. Scofield's deliberate purpose to put himself under obligation to the entire field of modern Bible study and scholarship. All through his labors on the Reference Bible he was consulting, either by correspondence or personal interview, the leading scholarly and spiritual Bible students of different lands. The destructive criticism and the new theology, both emanating from Germany, were in no sense congruous with his plan, and were wholly rejected as out of harmony with the great historic faith founded upon two thousand years of Christian experience and study.

The title-page of the Reference Bible gives the names of the consulting editors to whom, in the Introduction, the editor acknowledges special indebtedness and who worked with him in counsel, criticism, and guidance. These consulting editors were Henry G. Weston, D.D., LL.D. (deceased), President of Crozer Theological Seminary; James M. Gray, D.D., Dean of Moody Bible Institute; William J. Erdman, D.D., author of "The Gospel of John," etc.; W. G. Moorehead, D.D. (deceased), Professor in Xenia (U. P.) Theological Seminary; Elmore Harris, D.D. (deceased), President Toronto Bible Institute; Arno C. Gaebelein, author of "Harmony of Prophetic Word," etc.; Arthur T. Pierson, D.D. (deceased), author, editor, teacher. In addition to a great deal of correspondence with these consulting editors, three meetings of the group were held; and one can well imagine what interesting conferences these meetings must have been. The last of the three, reviewing the whole work, was held at Princeton, New Jersey, when several of the editorial board spent many days together, with access to the great theological library there.

In the remarkable introduction to the Reference Bible, which is, by a characteristic touch of the editor's unconventionality, labeled "(To be read)," Dr. Scofield says: "The editor disclaims originality. Other men have labored, he has but entered into their labors. The results of the study of God's Word by learned and spiritual men, in every division of the church and in every land, during the last fifty years, under the advantage of a perfected text, already form a vast literature, inaccessible to most Christian workers. The editor has proposed to himself the modest if laborious task of summarizing, arranging, and condensing this mass of material.

"That he has been able to accomplish this task at all is due in very large measure to the valuable suggestion sand co-operation of the consulting editors, who have freely given of their time and the treasures of their scholarship to this work. It is due to them to say that the editor alone is responsible for the final form of notes and definitions. The editor's acknowledgments are also due to a very wide circle of learned and spiritual brethren in Europe and America to whose labors he is indebted for suggestions of inestimable value. It may not be invidious to mention among these Prof. James Barrellet, of the Theological Faculty of Lausanne; Professors Sayce and Margoliouth, of Oxford; Mr. Walter Scott, the eminent Bible teacher; and Prof. C. R. Erdman, of Princeton.

"Finally, grateful thanks are due to those whose generous material assistance has made possible the preparation of a work involving years of time and repeated journeys to the centres of Biblical learning abroad."

It is to be remembered, therefore, that everything of importance in the Scofield Reference Bible represents the consensus of leading minds of Great Britain, the United States, and Canada, together with the treasures of Bible study worked out by similar students during the past century or so, as preserved in the best libraries of Europe and America. God led him to the right men; men who *lived* in Hebrew and Greek; and from these he eagerly received invaluable and judicious counsel. Going to Biblical centres abroad, he made sure that he gained possession of all the facts he needed to have. At Lausanne, Switzerland, for example, he reveled in the books in the great library there, a library begun by Calvin, some of whose books are still on its shelves.

Another statement in the Introduction of the Reference Bible is significant: "The last fifty years have witnessed an intensity and breadth of interest in Bible study unprecedented in the history of the Christian Church. Never before have so many reverent, learned, and spiritual men brought to the study of the Scriptures minds so free from merely controversial motive. A new and vast exegetical and expository literature has been created, inaccessible for bulk, cost, and time to the average reader. The winnowed and attested results of this half-century of Bible study are embodied in the notes, summaries, and definitions of this edition. Expository novelties and merely personal views and interpretations have been rejected."

Did the sojourns in Great Britain and elsewhere in Europe make any real contribution to the Scofield Reference Bible, apart from the opportunity they gave of freedom from interruption in the work? Could not this Reference Bible just as well have been made at home without stepping foot out of the United States? The question has been sincerely asked, and the facts here given answer it.

It is true that most of the explanatory and interpretative comment represents material that was familiar to the comparatively few soundly instructed and well-grounded students of the Word of God in our country and abroad. But the work done on the Scofield Reference Bible includes far more than this. It is a result that could have been produced only after an exhaustive study of books, and conferences with men, both friendly and unfriendly to the Word of God, both believing and unbelieving, both conservative and radical, so that every statement of the editor was finally made only after an intelligent and scholarly familiarity with the whole realm of modern Bible research. When a positive statement is made in the notes it is made in full recognition of the negative positions on that same point. All this made possible an orientation of the editor and gave the work a background, an atmosphere, a sometimes tacit evidence of familiarity with all view-points while presenting only the true view-point, which could never have been brought to pass without the travel and contact and research that went into it.

Those to whom the notes and references, the introductions and paragraph topics in the Scofield Reference Bible seem very simple—and they *are* simple and easy *reading*—do not always realize how much costly study and time and energy went into the mere deciding what to leave out. The editor read and read, and rejected and rejected, for *cause.* He had long personal interviews with Bible scholars with whom he fundamentally disagreed; but he drew out from them all that they could give him, and then went back to his constructive, not destructive, work, infinitely the better equipped. No man could sit in a pastor's study or a theological library in any one country alone and do this.

It will be remembered that the lifelong training and predisposition of Dr. Scofield, in literature and history and the law, had been making for the scholarly mind and the habits and methods of true scholarship. He had a magnificent Greek tutor away back in the days when he had been preparing to enter college. Later, after entering the Christian ministry, he made such progress in the study of the Bible tongues as was possible to a busy pastor. Despite the attainments thus acquired, Dr. Scofield, in his work upon the Reference Bible, always refused to settle any question linguistic in its nature upon his own conclusions unsupported by the great conservative authorities living and dead.

The scientific attitude of mind appears in this comment of Dr. Scofield: "If I find that I would *like* to have a word mean a certain thing, I pull up! 'Hold on, now,' I say to myself, 'I must see if it *does* mean that.' " And more than once, in making the Reference Bible, he spent a week on a single word, determined to know the facts before permitting himself to come to any conclusion.

An unexpected and very distinguished recognition of the learning and the scientific scholarship that have characterized Dr. Scofield's entire life, and that went into the making of the Reference Bible, was received in January of 1919 in a letter from the Société Académique d'Histoire Internationale, notifying Dr. Scofield of his election to membership. The late President of this Society, Frédéric Mistral, was one of the great poets of France. A medal of membership accompanied the election, and the following diploma, sent to Dr. Scofield, is a formal statement of the honor:

Société Académique d'Histoire Internationale
Fondée en 1903
Déclarée conformément à la Loi du
1er Juillet 1901—No. 154,142
50, Boulevard St. Jacques, 50, Paris
Président d'Honneur Perpétuel:
Mr. Frédéric Mistral
Commandeur de la Légion d'Honneur
Diplôme de Membre Fondateur décerne
à Monsieur le Dr. Cyrus I. Scofield
Paris, le 6 Février 1919

Le Président
Officier de la Légion d'Honneur
Vicomte de Faries

Le Secrétaire Général Officier
de l'Instruction Publique

There are, of course, certain merely theologically trained minds that never do, never can distinguish learning unless it is explained and couched in technical and impressive terms. Dr. Scofield came to the Bible with a mature mind, technically trained through the habit of close investigation. He studied the *Bible* for thirty years. He checked, verified, or corrected his own conclusions by conference with scholarly, Bible-saturated men of God, and by careful study of the writings of the saintly and spiritual as well as of the critical and unbelieving. Then, satisfied as to the conclusions of truth, he asked God that he might be simple, like the Bible itself, and make no display of what he calls "even the poor learning" that he himself might have. As a successful lawyer, he had been trained, especially in jury practice, to be simple and clear. He has never had any ambition to be impressive; he has had a great longing to help God's people and feed Christ's sheep. The result was the Scofield Reference Bible as it is to-day.

In spite of the modest disclaimer by the editor, and in spite of his frankly avowed and honestly maintained purpose to bring together for the benefit of the many the learning and research of the few, it must be remembered that the Scofield Reference Bible is by no means merely an eclectic work. It is also the ripe result of thirty years of unremitting personal study by its editor, whose methods, as have been seen, were utterly unusual in tracking down and digging out for himself, at no sparing of personal cost, under the direction of the Holy Spirit, the treasures of God's Word.

X

SATAN'S ATTACKS DEFEATED

Of course Satan tried desperately, over and over again, to block the work upon, and prevent the publishing of, a Reference Bible which he could see was going to mean regrettable inroads upon his domain in human lives. The attacks upon Dr. Scofield's bodily health were an indication of this; and during the stay at Oxford there were two more serious illnesses. But Satan can go only so far and no farther. The Lord intervened, and each time Dr. Scofield's health was restored and labors were resumed.

When a family problem in America required a cabled call to Mrs. Scofield to leave England for home, both she and her husband found spiritual fellowship and comfort in a little gathering of Plymouth Brethren with whom they had worshipped while in Oxford, and their Christian friends there interceded earnestly in their behalf. The day after special prayer in the meeting of the Plymouth Brethren concerning this matter, Dr. Scofield went with his wife to London and Liverpool, whence she started across the Atlantic on a Cunard steamship. After her boat was a day or two out at sea, another cablegram reached her husband, bringing the welcome news from home that the need had passed and all was well.

A page-proof of the New and Improved Edition of the Scofield Reference Bible, showing Dr. Scofield's corrections and comments.

A wireless message was at once flashed to the outgoing steamer and caught it six hundred miles at sea, so that Mrs. Scofield might have the good news before traveling farther. She was safeguarded all the way in her journey, and thus again an attempted interruption of Satan came to naught.

That summer Dr. Scofield rejoined his wife in America, and together they went on with the work at Lake Orion, Michigan; but he found it difficult to work there in view of the summer conferences at that well-known spot and the many interruptions sure to come to such a man as himself. So it was not long before they were again on their way across the ocean, this time for another and final stay in Switzerland, at Montreux.

It was on this second and last trip to Montreux, lasting eight or nine months, that the work on the Bible was actually finished. This was in the year 1907.

And now came another of those unmistakable attacks by Satan which he plainly hoped would prevent the giving of this work to the world.

The great books that had been slowly growing into finished copy for the printer—containing first the most accurate English Scripture text in existence, around which had been built up, little by little, and with infinite care and painstaking and lavish disregard of time, the results of a generation of personal study and the labors of a multitude of others,—were carefully packed in boxes by a carpenter in Montreux. These boxes were securely fastened by iron bands passing entirely around them, and they looked like the emigrants' boxes one often sees in the steerage of ocean steamers to be deposited at Ellis Island off New York. Dr. Scofield saw these put aboard the tender carrying baggage to the steamer which lay in the harbor at Boulogne.

The ocean voyage went by uneventfully. The steamer was

within one day of New York City when somehow Dr. Scofield felt strongly impressed with the desire to see if his precious boxes were safe in the baggage hold of the steamer.

With one of the steamship officers he went to satisfy himself. The boxes were not there.

With a sinking heart Dr. Scofield realized that the boxes might easily have been left in the tender, on the other side of the Atlantic, and then have been carried back to Boulogne. A new search was carefully made, without result. The baggage men were called in and the boxes were accurately described to them. They said that no such boxes had been put aboard with the luggage on this boat!

Now Dr. Scofield and his wife prayed earnestly together. And then it "occurred" to him that it might be worth while to search among the luggage of the emigrants in that boat. This search was now made, in the steerage, and there the boxes were found, safe and sound.

Notice this: if the boxes had not been looked for and located before the boat had reached New York, they would undoubtedly have been put off at Ellis Island with the luggage belonging to steerage passengers. There they would have been unclaimed, and they might never have been found. For Dr. Scofield, after reaching New York and finding that the boxes were not in the vessel in New York Harbor, would naturally have had Boulogne searched for them, and they would never have been found there. Satan's plans might have succeeded; but he is "an already defeated foe," and God only awaits our claiming his defeat, in simple faith in the name of Jesus, against every fresh attack that he makes.

When the precious copy for the new Bible was safely in America it was taken to Dr. Scofield's summer home near Northfield, at Ashuelot, New Hampshire. Here Dr. Scofield and his family were then living in primitive fashion, in tents, with one big tent as their living quarters. One Sunday morning—it was Mrs. Scofield's birthday—they were in one of the smaller tents when they heard a crackling noise. Hurrying out, they found the big tent a sheet of flames. But the manuscript of the Bible was not in that tent; it was in a little workshop near by. Had the wind been in the opposite direction, the precious manuscript could easily have gone up in smoke. But God was in charge, and again it was saved. It was too late to save the tent, and a great deal else; but Satan's fresh attempt against the manuscript was defeated.

And now the time was come for actually printing the great work. The type for the Bible was imported from the Clarendon Press in Oxford, England. Dr. and Mrs. Scofield went to New York and took apartments there, to insure close personal supervision of the work.

It was not best to let the big books containing the manuscript go all at once to the printers, so pages were cut from these books, and about twenty pages at a time were sent to the De Vinne Press for composition. As the proofs began to come back, Mrs. Scofield would act as "copyholder" to her husband, she reading aloud from the original copy, he carefully correcting the proof. This, of course, was after the proofreaders of the De Vinne Press had done their own careful work. During one of the hottest of summers, that of 1908, husband and wife toiled through this monumental labor for the Word of God. Their "day" was from about five o'clock in the morning until it was too dark to see at night. But they had long been at school in lessons of patience, and of painstaking, and of persistence.

One day a friend met Dr. Scofield in New York, by appointment, upon another matter, and they went together for a walk on Fifth Avenue. The friend asked concerning the progress of the work on the Reference Bible. Dr. Scofield abruptly came to a full stop in their walk as he said: "At eleven o'clock last night I came upon those impressive words, 'The End.' Yes, the work is finished—that is, in the sense in which any human work can ever be finished; for I am confident that there is only one work ever undertaken upon this earth which has in an absolute sense been finished, to which nothing can ever be added and from which nothing can ever be taken away. That is the finished work of Christ."

So the final proof was "passed." Then the eager waiting for the last sheets to come from the press, go to the binders, and come back the completed product. That day came; and with what gratitude to the Heavenly Father these two children of His handled their first copy of the Scofield Reference Bible, the reader who has followed this story of their God-planned, God-guided, God-illuminated, and God-energized work needs no writer's help to imagine.

XI

AS HIS FRIENDS KNOW HIM

It is a steep climb up the New Hampshire mountain roadway, severely testing the hill-climbing powers of an automobile, to get to "Crestwood," the summer home of Dr. C. I. Scofield at Ashuelot. But the hilltop view, after you have reached it, is worth the climb. From the house itself, and the garden round about it, one looks off over the beautiful Connecticut Valley with a sense of satisfying height, and distance, and sky and clouds and the glories of God's world. East Northfield, rich with memories of the ministry of D. L. Moody, is seen in the distance. Birds and flowers are round about in abundance. A bit of a cabin, a hundred yards or more from the house, forms a secluded study for Dr. Scofield, and there one finds chosen treasures of his rich library, marked and well-worn Bibles, and jottings on sermons and addresses.

There are evident reasons for the unusual catholicity of Dr. Scofield's temperament, interests, and relationships. Love of nature, love of men, love of scholarship, love of hard work, love of God and the Word of God—all these have combined to make the man as his friends know him. People who see him only as he has been ever since his conversion, with his simplicity of life and habits, would not realize that he was brought up in an extremely ritualistic way, as an Episcopalian. But this gives him a sympathy with that side of life that he might otherwise never have had. Yet when working on the monumental labor of his life, the Scofield Reference Bible, in Oxford, England, he and Mrs. Scofield found a welcome spiritual fellowship in a little group of Plymouth Brethren who worshipped there.

When this latter fact was mentioned in these biographical chapters as they were first published in the columns of *The Sunday School Times*, a Pennsylvania pastor-reader of that paper wrote to the biographer:

"This naturally raises the question: How far did Dr. Scofield and Mrs. Scofield share the peculiar beliefs of these people? On which of the many points which Plymouth Brethren set up to justify them in maintaining a separate denominational existence were they in accord?"

Dr. Scofield's own answer to this question will be read with interest by many:

"I am a minister of the Presbyterian Church, South, accepting in all sincerity the standards, and happy in the fellowship, of that branch of Presbyterianism, which seems to me very careful as to the doctrinal company it keeps in these easy days. But being such and so, I found it for certain personal reasons most convenient to worship usually while in Oxford with a little group of worthy middle-class Englishmen of the sect—they would warmly deny being a sect—of the so-called 'Open Brethren.' Just as in my widespread ministry I have worshipped with pretty nearly all of the other sects.

"I love the Baptists, but have never been asked, after a week in a Baptist pulpit: 'On which of the many points which Baptists set up to justify themselves in maintaining a separate denominational existence were Mrs. Scofield and myself in accord?' I gathered that

Dr. Scofield as He Is To-day

'Brethren' are emphatic for separatism—with their idea of which Mrs. Scofield and I are not in accord.

"But since every one of the Protestant sects had its origin in Separatism, based on doctrinal discord, mostly of the hair-splitting variety, and since Separatism was never once referred to in that simple, godly gathering in an old lumberyard office in Oxford, I no more felt constrained to raise the point than when I am worshipping with my Baptist, Methodist, or Dutch Reformed brethren. I have, indeed, had for many years an occasional happy Lord's day with the church of which this Pennsylvania reader is the justly esteemed pastor, and I do not to this day know to which branch, limb, or twig of our manifold Presbyterianism his great church belongs. But I love that church, and I love him."

And again—"You're a better Jew than I am," said a Jew to Dr. Scofield in all heartiness.

When he was asked recently what was his present denominational relationship, he wrote the following characteristic reply:

"I was ordained thirty-seven years ago as pastor of the First Congregational Church of Dallas, Texas. I remained in that pastorate until my removal to Northfield, Massachusetts, at the invitation of Mr. D. L. Moody and the First Congregational Church of that place. After seven years of happy work there, I resigned the active pastorate to begin the preparation of the Reference Bible and to finish the Correspondence Course.

"I had been aware that the Congregationalist denomination was rapidly changing its stand on certain doctrinal questions of great importance to my understanding of the Christian faith, but I am not controversial by nature, and was too intensely interested and occupied in Bible study to give close attention to current discussions. And so it happened that, at last, I lifted my face from my work and found that the denomination, in whose fellowship I have found great and true men of God, had resolutely moved to positions to which I could not follow. It was, therefore, heartening to look about me and find that I was in the very midst of a people to whom the old definitions, the old methods of expression, sufficed— the Southern Presbyterian Church. I reflected that they were the very people who, equally with the Congregationalists, knew me best, and I asked the Paris, Texas, Presbytery of that denomination to take me into its membership. And they did, with many gratifying expressions of welcome, and there I have been restful and happy.

"There is not a trace of bitterness in my heart in all this, for my memory holds too many instances of kind things said and done by my Congregationalist brothers to leave any room for anything but gratitude and esteem; but it remains true that the designation 'Congregationalist' would not now describe me. It stands for certain liberties which I do not allow myself, and for a certain attitude toward the Bible and historic Christianity which is not my attitude."

There is something in Dr. Scofield that draws people close to him. As a veteran of the Confederate Army, having fought through the Civil War, he surprised certain people in Dallas, Texas, during his memorable pastorate in that great Southern State. On a certain Memorial Day he was invited to speak to the veterans of the local "Camp" of Confederates. And about the same time he was asked if he would address, on that Memorial Day, the local Post of the Grand Army of the Republic. This would have seemed a dilemma to some men. But Pastor Scofield went to the heads of each of these organizations and asked whether there would be any objection to having the members of both associations of veterans meet together, in his church, for a joint service. Those in charge said there would be no objection, though some doubt was expressed as to whether the men would come. But when the invitation was extended the men did indeed come, in two separate bodies, and the meeting was splendidly attended. Scofield gave a straightforward message, including the Gospel; and as a result of that service some of the veterans, meeting with this true pastor in his study afterward, were led to the Lord Jesus Christ as their Saviour. And joint meetings of the Confederate and the Union veterans have been continued since that time on Memorial Day.

One of the first impressions I ever had of Dr. Scofield was as to the ease with which people could get to him. It was at the time of the great Prophetic Conference held in Chicago in February of 1914, less than six months before the storm of the world war broke. He gave a fearless Scriptural message on the assurance in God's Word that world-wide and permanent peace can never come save by the coming of the Prince of Peace, though that message was laughed at by the general public and newspaper reporters at that time. I think this was the first time I had ever seen or heard Dr. Scofield, and I hoped I might get his autograph in my personal copy of the Scofield Reference Bible.

At the close of one of his addresses I sought him out, and found that others had the same desire. And I supposed that a man of his prominence, so much in demand for public addresses, must be more or less annoyed by the importunity of strangers coming to him and "bothering" him for an autograph. Even then he was about to leave the church to catch a train. But he greeted every individual who came up to him at the close of that meeting, even as he greeted me, then an entire stranger, as though we were all doing him a personal favor by letting him write in our Bibles! I think I have never seen such genuine courtesy and unaffected Christian love in a conference speaker or Bible teacher as I saw in him at that time, and as I have seen in him many times since.

When Dr. Scofield was at Northfield one of the students served him as his "chore boy." That student is now pastor of a church in New England, the Rev. Robert Clark, of Lyndon, Vermont; and his tribute to Dr. Scofield confirms what so many others have come to know of the man. Mr. Clark writes:

"I was intimately acquainted with him when he was president of the Northfield Bible Training School. From 1900 to 1903 the school was open to men; I attended it during these years. That I loved and revered the doctor as a teacher goes without saying. He is my spiritual father, and I owe to him, under God, more than I owe to any other man. He brought me into the light and liberty of the Gospel, and gave me methods of Bible study that have proved fruitful ever since.

"But I was even more closely associated with the doctor than as a student, for I worked for him for a year as his 'chore boy,' and spent the summer with him at his summer camp. During that time I was much in his company, driving him to his appointments, or to the train, or riding out in the afternoons. In this way I came to know him very well, and I can truly say that the closer contact deepened my love and respect for him.

"I found that Dr. Scofield was a *companionable* man. He never seemed to feel any distance between himself, the man of wide experience, and a raw country youth; he talked as freely to me as to his guests. He was always ready to give me aid and to clear up some difficulty in my Bible study.

"I found that Dr. Scofield was a *humble* man. He was teachable. He was as ready to listen to the experience of the humblest believer as to the mature saint, and he believed that he could learn from both.

"I found that Dr. Scofield was a *man of prayer*. He prayed about everything, the little things as well as the big things: all were carried to the throne of grace. Two things in this connection made a deep impression on me.

"In the doctor's study, when I agreed to stay with him for the summer, we knelt down and he prayed for God's blessing on our relations as master and servant.

"One morning, when I went over to the family tent to get orders for the day, I heard him praying. I paused, and I heard my name mentioned; he was praying for me, that I might have a pleasant trip down to the village. That was characteristic of his life and practice."

This man who has helped such countless multitudes loves to commend others who are helping their fellows. He one time wrote a letter to the office of *The Sunday School Times*, speaking with discriminating and hearty appreciation of the special writing that was being done, in different departments of that paper, by various members of its staff. Then he added:

"Thank God for the gifts, but how important to remember that while the Holy Spirit makes gifted Christians, 'dividing to every man severally as he will,' yet it is the blessed Lord who assigns the place of service of the men thus endowed. And just as there is no self-choice of gift, so there is no self-choice of the place and sphere of service in the gift. When I find a man ministering *His* gift, in the right *place*, I'm just happy—oh, yes, and HELPED."

Dr. Scofield loves all nature—not only men and women and children, but the whole created world, still so beautiful in spite of what Satan and sinners have done to mar God's work. I recall how he once pointed to a glowing, blazing bed of poppies, and asked if I did not think their brilliant color was wonderful against the dark green of the fields and the trees in the background.

A little bird bath has been cut from the natural stone, just outside the "Crestwood" house, for the countless little friends of the air that the Scofields love.

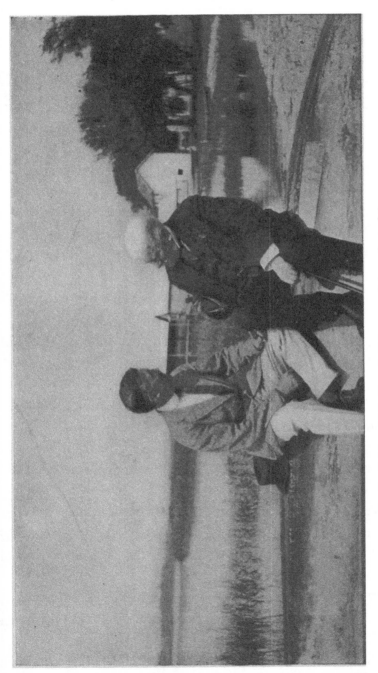

Dr. Scofield and Mr. Trumbull in a special session of the Southfield Bible Conference, Crescent City, Florida.

And to hear Dr. Scofield talk about St. Francis of Assisi, in his love of nature, is a memorable experience. He read aloud to us page after page from that old Christian's writings, dwelling upon the nature-love there. Thus: "This perfect lover of poverty [St. Francis] permitted one luxury—he even commanded it at Portiuncula—that of flowers; the Brother was bidden not to sow vegetables and useful plants only; he must reserve one corner of good ground for 'our sisters, the flowers of the fields.' Francis talked with them also, or rather he replied to them, for their mysterious and gentle language crept into the very depth of his heart."

In a Bible study on the fourteenth chapter of John's Gospel Dr. Scofield has said, commenting on our Lord's words, "I go to prepare a place for you": "He is giving me an experience of it in this beautiful world of variety. Why should I want to live in a marble mansion cold and fine? I want to live in nature, in a place which exactly responds to my complex nature." And it is a conviction of his that we shall find heaven filled with such beauties as God has already given to us in the world of nature so lovingly provided for His children now and here, only, of course, then infinitely more beautiful and more wonderful.

No one who is as *human* as this man of God could be lacking in a keen sense of humor. And no one can long be with Dr. Scofield without finding contagious evidences of his love of fun and of wit. Like all persons who really enjoy humor, he can see a joke on himself as well as on others. He tells one such, which occurred when he was preaching at a conference. His son was a little fellow of five or six years at that time, and insisted on sitting on the platform with his father. For a while the youngster played quietly with his father's watch, which had been given to him to keep him quiet. Then, without warning, the boy crossed the platform and handed the watch to his father, who was in the midst of his sermon.

Dr. Scofield was by no means near the conclusion of his address, but, to the surprise of the presiding officer, he hastily closed his message. When asked later about the abruptness with which he had brought his sermon to an end, he explained that he thought his allotted time was up, and that his young son had been sent in this way to inform him!

He likes to tell of an experience he had when he was a private in the Confederate Army, and had gone off with some fellow-soldiers to rob an apple orchard. As they were in the midst of their looting, a Confederate officer passed down the road, and, looking across the fence into the orchard, asked the boys what they were doing. There was nothing to answer, except to explain that they were helping themselves to the apples; and they stood in fear and trembling as to what would come next. The officer drew his sword, passed it over the fence to young Scofield, and said laconically, "Spear me one, will you?" The relief was intense.

Another Confederate reminiscence which appeals to Dr. Scofield's sense of humor is in connection with a formal dinner that he attended, to which Senator Roscoe Conkling had been invited. The Senator failed to appear until quite late, and then came, in immaculate evening dress of course, to join the rest who had been expectantly waiting his arrival. "In his oracular and ponderous way," says Dr. Scofield, "the great statesman explained his delay: 'The senior Senator from Massachusetts [Sumner] has just been making his annual attempt to enact a law to abolish the distinction made by God Almighty between black and white.' "

Readers of *The Sunday School Times* may recall a characteristic letter from Dr. Scofield, written to the Editor at the time the latter's church was looking for a new pastor. A high standard both of orthodoxy and of pastoral abilities was set up by that church; and Dr. Scofield wrote about the matter as follows:

"Is it faith, or is it presumption in this pagan age, for your dear church to ask so much of the ministry of the day? I have read, of course, with perfect delight the resolutions of your church as to the faith necessary to be held by the pastor whom you seek. But when I look upon the ministry of the day and the material actually at hand, I am dismayed and overwhelmed by the contrast. The coming of the Lord draws near, and we shall soon have with us again the Apostle Paul—I would put him first among those whom I would recommend, and I can think of no other who would fill all these requisites, considering I myself have passed the age of pastoral work."

Deepest intensity of conviction is as characteristic of this man as his lighter and tenderer side. Those who attended one of the Bible conferences at Crescent City, Florida, in recent years may recall the vehemence with which Dr. Scofield said one day from the platform, speaking of the tragic devastation that the Higher Criticism has wrought among the ministers of this generation: "I would rather spend Sunday morning in a saloon than sitting in a church under the preaching of a modern Higher Critic!"

Looking back over his own lifetime experiences, this veteran saint says there have been two great epochs in his own life. "The first was when I ceased to take as final human teachings about the Bible and went to the Book itself. The second was when I found Christ as Victory and Achievement."

His study and teaching of the Victorious Life have blessed many. His epigrammatic putting of this truth goes to the heart of it: "Christian experience, and the experience of the Christian, may be two very different things." By this Dr. Scofield is reminding us that normal "Christian experience" of the New Testament sort is always victorious. But the experience of many a Christian is anything but victorious. For "Christian experience is wholly the result of the Producer of Christian experience—the Holy Spirit." And this Bible teacher has rendered a great service in insisting that every Christian has the Victorious Life. For the Victorious Life is simply Christ Himself; and every Christian has Christ—or else he is not a Christian; "if any man have not the Spirit of Christ, he is none of his" (Romans 8:9). But many a Christian who, because he is a Christian, has Christ indeed within his heart, is yet failing to yield wholly to Christ and to believe wholly in His sufficiency, and therefore is sadly failing to have a personal experience of victory over sin. Because he has Christ he has the "Victorious Life," but he is not letting that Life, or Christ, work in overcoming power. In other words, this is the oft-repeated counsel that the Christian "possess his possessions," and believe in and enjoy the "all things" that God has given him in Christ Jesus (1 Corinthians 3:21).

In ceasing to take as final human teachings about the Bible, and in going to the Book itself, Dr. Scofield has labored for many years in the spirit of the true scholar. That always means the drudgery of infinite care and tedious painstaking. As this Life Story has pointed out, Scofield as a boy and a young man, before he ever knew the Lord, was given of God a temperament and a habit of work that may well be described by that definition of "the scholarly temperament—that rare combination of profound insight, sustained attention, microscopic accuracy, iron tenacity, and disinterested pursuit of truth, which characterizes the great scientific discoverer or the great historian." It was some thirty years of this sort of study, research, and hard work that made the Scofield Reference Bible what it is to-day in clearness, dependableness, simplicity, and compactness. Writing to a friend about these chapters in his Life Story, after they had been appearing in the columns of *The Sunday School Times*, Dr. Scofield said: "Charles started in with the word 'amazing' as characterizing a life which seems to me chiefly one of drudgery, but now I am 'amazed' to see how skilfully he makes my very drudgery interesting." Drudgery is always interesting—to other people who look on! Only the few find it interesting enough to go in for it themselves, and to keep at it, in season and out of season, until the work is really done.

But with these characteristics of what may be called the sternly scientific make of mind, the brilliant insight into truth, lucid simplicity of statement, and powers that have made this man a marked character whether in the world or in the Church of Christ, there are also a simplicity and a faith that are childlike in their beauty and tenderness.

His love of St. Francis of Assisi has already been mentioned. He told a little group of friends one day that he counted St. Francis his own particular saint. And then he went on to explain that, as some one else has said, everybody ought to have a special saint—"not to take the place of Christ, of course, but to interpret Christ *down* to *me*. As Paul says, 'Be ye followers of me *even* as I am of Christ'—but test me by Christ every time, Paul was careful to urge."

St. Francis' love of birds "found" Dr. Scofield. With deep feeling he read aloud this passage from "Sabatier's Life of St. Francis": "Full of joy, he was going on his way when, perceiving some flocks of birds, he turned aside a little from the road to go to them. Far from taking flight, they flocked around him as if to bid him welcome. 'Brother birds,' he said to them then, 'you ought to praise and love your Creator very much. He has given you feathers for clothing, wings for flying, and all that is needful for you. He has made you the noblest of his creatures; he permits you to live in the pure air; you have neither to sow nor to reap, and yet he takes care of you, watches over you, and guides you.' Then the birds began to arch their necks, to spread out their wings, to open their beaks, to look at him, as if to thank him, while he went up and down in their midst stroking them with the border of his tunic, sending them away at last with his blessing." After reading this Dr. Scofield said quietly: "I believe that if we were filled with the Holy Spirit the birds would come close to us."

"Abba, Father," says Dr. Scofield, "is the affectionate realization of God's fatherhood. And so one exclaims, in a flood of tenderness and love, 'Oh, Father!' or, 'Dear Father.' This is said, of course, only in the Spirit. But how commentators have bothered and puzzled over that expression, 'Abba, Father.' "

The depth and simplicity of Dr. Scofield's faith come out in the comment he has made on the narrative, in the "Life of St. Francis," of that godly man's healing of a loathsome leper. The story is a beautiful one, and after reading it aloud to friends Dr. Scofield said, with enthusiasm: "Well, now, that doesn't stumble me. It would be strange if such a man could not heal lepers, by the power of God."

The beauty of true Christian mysticism is recognized in his comment on this saint: "Francis is of the race of the mystics, for no intermediary comes between God and his soul." Christian mysticism, he points out, is what has been called "immediacy"— that is, that nothing, not even prayer, is needed to bring the believer into the presence of God. This is certainly the teaching of the New Testament concerning the union with Christ which is true of all Christian believers. Not nearness, but *union*. We are not *with* Christ, but *in* Christ; he is not *with* us, but *in* us. Tennyson knew this when he wrote,

> "Closer is He than breathing, and
> nearer than hands and feet."

Dr. Scofield's childlike trust in God's love and the sufficiency of God's grace to give His children anything comes out in the story he tells of a personal experience of answered prayer. Some good Christian people would quite misunderstand this story—unless they heard Dr. Scofield himself tell it, and saw the light in his face, the irresistible humor in his smile, and the Christian faith back of it.

With his advancing years he very much wished for an automobile. He was telling a minister friend about this one time, and how, with his desire for a car, he decided to pray for it. "And," he went on, "God heard my prayer and answered it, and he sent me an automobile."

"Is that so?" said the minister who was listening to the experience. "I never thought of praying for an automobile," the minister continued. "But as I think of it, I believe I could be of greater service to the Lord, in the Christian ministry, if I had one. I could use my time to better advantage; I could make more pastoral calls; I could get more work done. I believe I may start praying for one myself."

And then Dr. Scofield, as he tells the incident to-day with a twinkle in his eye, surprised his minister friend. "Well," he said quietly, "if you believe that you could render better service as a Christian minister with an automobile, and believe that you ought to ask God for it for that purpose, you do so. But I didn't ask God for an automobile in order to render better service. I told God that I had worked pretty hard all my life, and that I was getting on in years, and that I wanted an automobile as a toy, a plaything, something in which to rest and enjoy myself. And God sent it to me."

Whether the minister saw the point is not recorded. But that there is a point there, and a very real one for God's children, cannot be doubted. God loves to give his children good times. But how few of his children really believe this!

Many a friend has had reason to know of the great tenderness of heart in this man of God. He has a genius for friendship; the light that comes into his eyes as he greets a friend is wonderful. Even those who have been new-comers in his circle of acquaintances notice this. I remember seeing him, one day, walking up the street when he did not know that I was near him. As he walked along he noticed coming toward him a man whom he had only recently met. Dr. Scofield stopped short, lifted up his head, reached out his hand to his acquaintance, and a great light of friendship shone on his face as he spoke to this man whom he had already taken into his heart.

We were talking together one day, in his rustic study out under the trees in the New Hampshire summer home, and he had been speaking of all that belongs to the believer, in Christ. As he came to the close of what he was saying, he added, "And then we come to the ineffable—!" He stopped, and a radiant smile broke over his face. His eyes closed, and without any further word he prayed quietly: "We thank thee, O Father, that Jesus does it all."

GREYSHINGLES

Dispensational Publishing House is striving to become the go-to source for Bible-based materials from the dispensational perspective.

Our goal is to provide high-quality doctrinal and worldview resources that make dispensational theology accessible to people at all levels of understanding.

Visit our blog regularly to read informative articles from both known and new writers.

And please let us know how we can better serve you.

Dispensational Publishing House, Inc.
Taos, NM 87571

DispensationalPublishing.com

CPSIA information can be obtained
at www.ICGtesting.com
Printed in the USA
LVHW090035081119
636699LV00001B/1/P